Thriving
AS A THERAPIST

The Ultimate Guide to Building and Scaling Your Business for Freedom, Joy, and Financial Abundance

Megan Gunnell, LMSW
Founder
Thriving Well Institute

Thriving Well Institute

© 2023 by Megan Gunnell

All rights reserved. No part of this book may be used or reproduced in any manner whatsoever without written permission, except in the case of brief quotations in critical articles and reviews. For more information, please contact info@thrivingwellinstitute.com

Published 2023

Printed in the United States of America

ISBN: 979-8-218-18132-1

PRAISE FOR
THRIVING AS A THERAPIST

"Megan Gunnell is helping therapists build a life beyond the walls of a traditional therapy setting. Thriving as a Therapist *doesn't just give you the business skills you didn't learn in school, it gives you the tools to build a life you love.*"

—Jake Ernst, MSW RSW, Therapist & Writer @mswjake

"As someone who works with many therapists professionally, I'm often struck by how many are burned out by the profession and how broken the business model is. Megan Gunnell is here to help fix all that! In Thriving as a Therapist, Megan guides therapists through the breakthrough model that works for her and the thousands of therapists who've put her wisdom into action. No more going it alone and pushing through. Readers will have a step by step plan with clear practices, built in support, models for scaling and helping more people—without wearing themselves out. In fact, this is the book to empower therapists with renewal, abundance, fulfillment and joy."

—Lisa Tener, book coach and award-winning author of *The Joy of Writing Journal*

"Megan Gunnell has a deep caring for her fellow therapists and a clear sense of how to help them thrive. No matter where you live or what your situation, this book will help you find your path forward to unlock the personal and financial freedom you deserve."

—Jennie Schottmiller, LMFT, CPA Founder of Simple Profit

"*Thriving as a Therapist is a must-read for anyone in the field, regardless of their career stage. With its practical insights and actionable advice, this book is the ultimate roadmap for therapists looking to build a thriving practice, create multiple streams of income, and navigate the challenges of building and scaling a business. This book serves as a testament to her wisdom and expertise, providing a comprehensive guide for therapists seeking to grow and thrive in their profession.*"

—Kym Tolson, LCSW, The Traveling Therapist

"*Mandatory reading for every mental health graduate student, and everyone who ever was a grad student,* Thriving as a Therapist *is a textbook on how to be the best possible therapist in the profession. Megan Gunnell lays out a blueprint for success in the professional mental health field, as well as how to stretch beyond the therapy couch to serve the world in bigger and more profound ways. Packed with her own insights and step by step guidance, this book will help everyone from the brand new grad to the seasoned veteran live their dream life in the mental health field without losing their own mental health along the way.*"

—Dr. Amy Parks, LPC, ACS – Founder, Clinical Supervision Directory

"*If you've ever been a part of Megan's Facebook group, online membership, courses, retreats, or summits, you know that she is thorough, thoughtful, and fun. This book is no different. She takes you through the steps of building a private practice to create a business (and life as a clinician) that you'll love. As always, you are in great hands with Megan's guidance.*"

—Tina Kocol, LPC, CGP Founder of Philly EMDR and Green Circle Collective. Author of *The Perfectionism Journal*

"*Thriving as a Therapist* is a must read for every therapist in private practice! Megan leads by example in the way she lives her life and runs her businesses. Her book walks you through the practical steps to scale a private practice and also live your best life. You don't need to sacrifice your mental health to thrive as a therapist. In fact, the world needs you to succeed and Megan's book will help you do so with more joy and freedom."

—Uriah Guilford, LMFT, author of *The Productive Practice*

"Megan is freaking brilliant. We all know it is not enough to just grow a therapy practice. You can grow and be out of balance with your life and grow in a way that does not allow you to scale. Being a therapist is easy... being a profitable therapist is not. That's why I love Megan's book. It is full of actionable ideas and strategies to help ANY therapist grow and scale, not only their business but their life!!"

—Rachel Miller, Organic Traffic Strategist at Moolah Marketing

"Megan strikes the very fine balance between supporting clinicians in their clinical work and helping them dream bigger, beyond the therapy room. There's no one I trust more than Megan to guide therapists along their entire journey in practice, no matter what path they choose."

—Anna Walker, Founder and CEO, Walker Strategy Co.

"If you're a therapist who wants to thrive (or just needs that reminder that you DESERVE to), this is the book for you! Megan's words effortlessly warm your heart and help give you the drive you deserve as a therapist. This book is packed with real, raw, and inspiring information to have you gain the knowledge and insights needed as a therapist to grow. Megan leads from the soul and this book shows it. A true must read for any therapist in the field."

—Andrea Brognano, Founder of Achieve with Andrea

"Working with Megan not only transformed my business, she changed my life. Megan is an expert in helping therapists realize the bigger impact they can have besides doing direct client work, in a way that's genuine, comforting, and knowledgeable. This is the playbook therapists need in order to scale their practice successfully."

—Gabrielle Juliano-Villani, Founder of GJV Consulting

"*Thriving as a Therapist* is a much-needed guidebook for aspiring private practice clinicians. Megan's authenticity and practicality empower readers to think through not only how they will start their practice, but also how they can build a career that is sustainable long-term. I was surprised by how much information Megan was able to share concisely, with clarity, and a fair bit of humor. She provides a compelling vision of a full career; from your first client in solo practice to thriving as an entrepreneur with multiple income streams. Thanks, Megan, for this book and for your mentorship of the next generation of therapists!"

—Katie Vernoy, LMFT, Co-founder, Therapy Reimagined and Co-Host of The Modern Therapist's Survival Guide podcast

"*Thriving as a Therapist* is a must read for any therapist new or established in the field. This book provides a wealth and depth of information that they do not teach you in graduate school. Thriving as a Therapist is like a master class with a friend who has been in the field for years. It's concise, comprehensive and conversational. This book will help take the fear out of thriving for a field of helpers."

—Sarah Watson, LPC & CST, Founder of Simple Sex Education and Sarah Watson PLLC

"Megan provides valuable information in this book to help you grow and thrive as a therapist. Her authenticity allows you to feel seen, valued, and motivated for growth. You will be able to see a future that goes beyond the one on one client sessions and promotes an environment of thriving instead of barely surviving."

—Ashley Hubbard, MS, NCC, LPC, LMHC, Founder & Director of Vibrant Journey Counseling, PLLC

"Megan is an incredibly impressive business owner. As well as being accomplished and experienced, she is smart, thoughtful and warm. I love how she supports fellow therapists and how she truly lives the ethos that she shares with us. If you're looking for someone to guide you in developing your own meaningful and abundant business, these are the qualities to look for. Thank you Megan, for the ideas and guidance you share so generously."

—Tamara Howell MSc, PGDip, Reg. BACP (Accred.)

"This is one of the most comprehensive books for therapists to date. Thriving as a Therapist is a go to book for therapists looking to start a private practice and a book for established therapists who are looking to diversify their services beyond 1:1 work. This gem of a book will get your wheels turning on how to build the business of your dreams."

—Maureen Werrbach, Founder of The Group Practice Exchange

To every therapist who wants to thrive,
this book is for you.

FEAR

By Kahlil Gibran

*It is said that before entering the sea
a river trembles with fear.*

*She looks back at the path she has traveled,
from the peaks of the mountains,
the long winding road crossing forests and villages.*

*And in front of her,
she sees an ocean so vast,
that to enter
there seems nothing more than to disappear forever.*

*But there is no other way.
The river can not go back.*

*Nobody can go back.
To go back is impossible in existence.*

*The river needs to take the risk
of entering the ocean
because only then will fear disappear,
because that's where the river will know
it's not about disappearing into the ocean,
but of becoming the ocean.*

CONTENTS

Introduction to Section 1—Building Your Business   **15**
    1   Setting Up Your Business   25
    2   Marketing Your Practice   33
    3   Building Your Referral Network   45
    4   Practice Management—Setting Your Fees, Setting Up Your Policies   51
    5   Define Your Niche, Establish Your Authority and Expertise   61
    6   Money and Entrepreneurial Mindset   67

Introduction to Section 2—Scaling Your Business   **75**
    7   Building Groups   79
    8   Hosting Retreats   91
    9   Creating Online Courses   107
    10   Building a Group Practice   119
    11   Pivoting to Coaching   131
    12   Speaking Gigs   139
    13   Outsourcing and Hiring a Team   147
    14   Building a Platform   155

Introduction to Section 3—Thriving   **169**
    15   Self-Care   173
    16   Creativity & Play   181
    17   Boundaries, Gratitude, Mindfulness   187
    18   I Believe in You!   197

Acknowledgments   203
Book Club Discussion Questions   205
About the Author   209

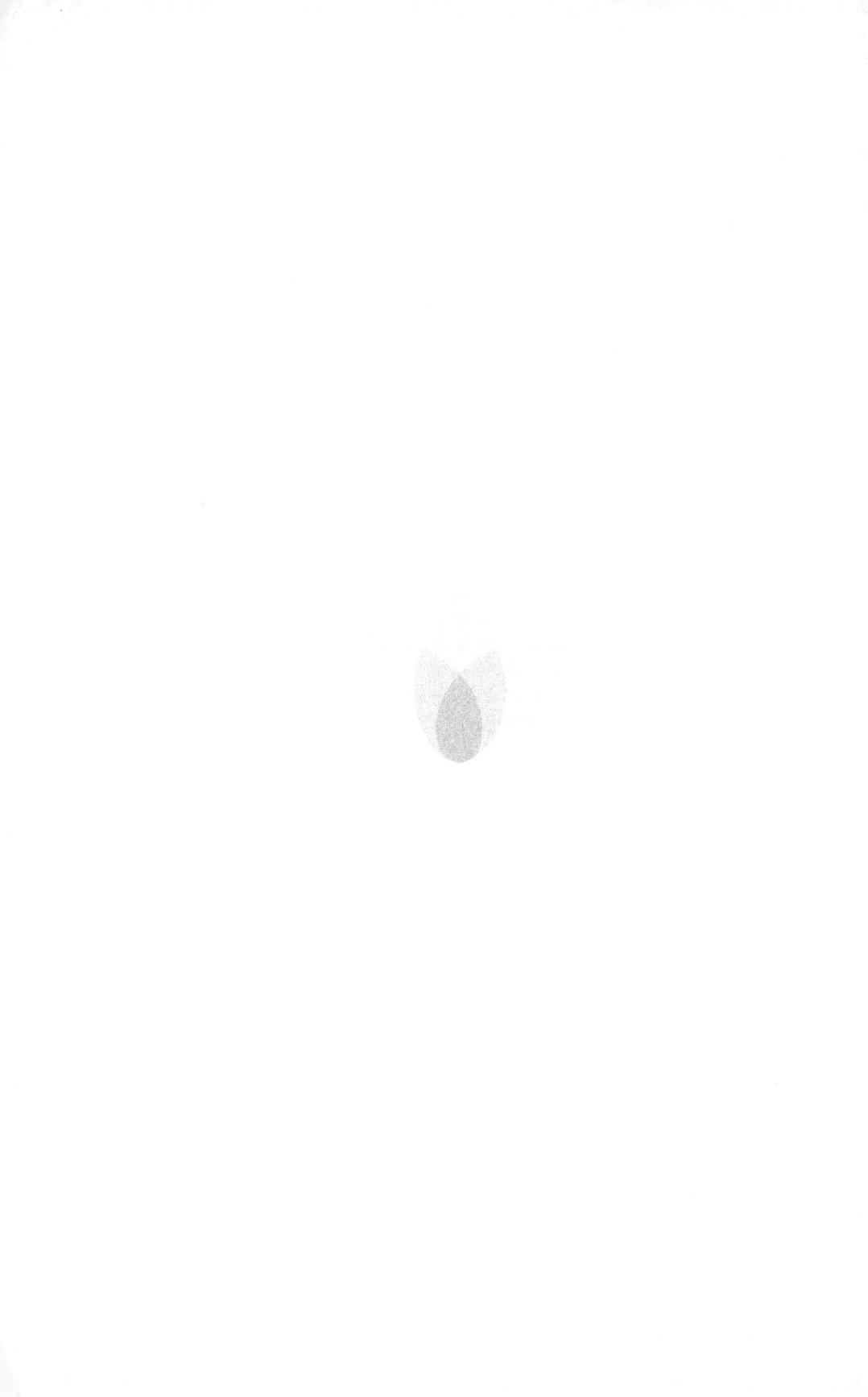

INTRODUCTION TO SECTION 1
Building Your Business

WATCH VIDEO:

Megan Gunnell introduces
Thriving as a Therapist

https://www.thrivingwellinstitute.com/book.html

The doors opened to the inpatient psych ward. It was family visiting hours, and we walked down the white hospital corridor toward a big open rec room. I've always hated bright, sterile overhead lighting, and maybe this is why. I didn't want to be there. I didn't want to be visiting my dad. The patients were stamping letters into leather bands for their rec therapy activity. The smell of the leather is seared in my mind. My dad looked up and, in one moment, appeared both relieved and ashamed.

My dad was making me a bracelet out of a wide strip of leather. A bracelet I would hide deep in the bottom of my jewelry box. One I would never wear for fear someone would ask me where I got it.

My dad's tremor upset me. Everything about this afternoon upset me. What he was wearing. The fact he was there. The other patients. The feeling of uncertainty—when would he be able to leave, why was the unit locked, what did he do to make him end up here, why did my parents get divorced?

> *My friends had "normal" dads. Dads who coached their sports teams. Dads who wore suits to work and took business trips. Dads who helped fix up the house and read the newspaper on Sunday mornings.*
>
> *Visiting hours were done, and it was time to go home. I also felt relief and shame.*

Mental illness at the core creates a vast sense of "otherness"—a sense of difference and that we don't belong. Like many therapists, I found myself wanting to become a therapist because of my own family history.

All I ever wanted to do was build a practice, be my own independent boss, help my clients, and fill my caseload. I had endless compassion for my clients because I understood what they were feeling. I had shared, lived experiences that made their situations relatable to me.

I bookended grad school with babies. Something I would not recommend doing! When I graduated with my Master of Social Work (MSW) from the University of Michigan School of Social Work, I gave the graduation speech to my class while pregnant with my second born and when my son was just three and a half years old. I busted out twenty-page papers at night when my son was sleeping. I nibbled on saltine crackers to curb my morning sickness all the way to Ann Arbor on my forty-five-minute commute to school. It wasn't easy, and when I was done, I wanted to dive headfirst into building my private practice.

But there were no coaches. No courses. No guidance. We had zero training on business development in grad school. I knew nothing about being an entrepreneur. I didn't even understand how to open a business bank account.

Hugely pregnant and totally unaware of how to begin, I walked into the waiting room of a group practice near my home. I introduced myself to the receptionist, who was warm and friendly. I asked to speak with the director, Diane, and I scheduled a meeting with her. She was a quiet, older, single woman who seemed surprised by my energy to get started, especially considering I looked ready to give birth in her lobby.

I begged her to let me join their group practice, saying I was willing to beat the bushes for referrals and that I would take any overflow clients any therapist there had to give me. I didn't need my own office; I would float to any office that wasn't being used at the time. I was willing to take walk-ins or cold calls. I was willing to take sliding scale clients and go very low on my rates just to fill my caseload and get more experience.

I knew I had to work toward completing my hours for my full license, and I felt the pressure of the ticking clock with my delivery approaching.

But I had always pictured being a therapist in private practice.

I saw myself greeting my clients in the waiting room and walking them back to the therapy room, which was like a little sacred, confidential place where they could share their innermost thoughts and feelings. A warm, safe container where all feelings were welcomed and encouraged. An ultra private place only for the therapist and client. I'd have a white noise machine humming outside the door. Soft lighting with lamps only—no overhead lights allowed. I'd have live plants that I would lovingly tend to between visits. A beautiful mug for my favorite cup of hot cinnamon tea. A never-ending supply of Kleenex, a small wastebasket, and a clean desk.

I pictured a comfortable living room space with a soft velvet couch and cozy armchairs. Soft impressionist paintings of flowers or natural scenes. A couple of clocks so both me and my client could notice the time we had left in each session. A warm rug, a few small side tables, and a mirror close to the door so clients could check themselves before leaving if they had a particularly tearful session.

The feeling of this vision was calming, intimate, supportive, professional, warm, and engaging. There was also a feeling of heft. It was the weight of holding space. I could feel it in my arms, like an anchor, holding steadfast for whatever choppy waters my clients brought to session. This weight would envelop them subconsciously like heavy walls around a big box with something super precious inside. Inside this office, they could unpack whatever they wanted. They could pull out the contents of their innermost fears, memories, hopes, dreams, darkness, sadness, longings, wishes, and expectations, and in this process discover their deepest insights, knowings, and wisdom.

This is what I envisioned.

This is what I held onto that day when I ventured out to start my practice.

Once Diane said yes, I somehow thought that the biggest hurdle was behind me! I remember going home that night thinking I had done it. I had officially started a practice.

But sadly, I had not.

I'd just secured the right to pay for office space, and despite being pregnant, saddled with a mountain of grad school debt, and totally broke, I was on the hook for that monthly rent whether or not I had any clients.

Unafraid of most challenges and born with ambition, I dove in headfirst. Not knowing how to build a marketing plan or how to build my referral network, I woke up the next morning in a bit of a panic. I decided to put on work clothes, head into the office, and start to observe how this was done.

The receptionist looked a little surprised to see me. I had no clients and I hadn't scheduled any office space. I started to befriend her. I wanted to understand everything about how it worked to run a practice, and I knew she was at the center of it all. Therapists came rushing in the back door, flipped on their lights and sound machines, walked briskly past the reception desk, and greeted their clients one after the other. Hour by hour, doors opened and closed, opened and closed. More clients came and went and therapists moved in and out quickly, grabbing client files from the massive filing cabinet, slamming the drawer shut with their hip, refreshing their water, coffee, and tea, then picking up the next client and heading back into session.

This was my first clue.

It appeared that the most "successful therapists" with busy caseloads did not have time to gingerly contemplate their work between visits. There was no time for lovingly tending to their live plants or making sure their desk was clean. They were flipping clients like short-order cooks. Depression, anxiety, bipolar, addiction—next in line, order up.

I was impressed with how many clients were seen in one day. I spent a little time in one of the empty offices by myself. Maybe waiting for a miraculous walk-in client or a chat with a therapist who had a no-show or cancellation. Mostly I just sat in silence looking around at the decor that another therapist had picked out.

I noticed the dust on all the surfaces. The messy desk, Post-it Notes, pens, and cough drops all over. I noticed the full trash can and tissue boxes. I moved around the office sort of feeling out each seat and position. What would it feel like to sit in the therapist's chair? What about at their desk? What would it feel like to sit where the client sat—right in that soft spot on the couch where over the course of years and years, hundreds, if not thousands, of clients had sat?

I noticed the amazing array of self-help and clinical books on the bookshelf in these offices. A wealth of knowledge I had not even cracked the spine on yet. I ran my finger over the spines and realized how little I really knew despite finishing a graduate degree on the subject.

Suddenly, I felt totally overwhelmed.

I felt like I was at the very bottom of the mountain. What a stark contrast to feeling so accomplished and hopeful at graduation. I felt like I'd just finished climbing Mt. Everest only to look up and realize I had not even started yet.

What did I just do?

I'd just spent thousands of dollars on a degree that I couldn't even use yet. I had a three-and-a-half-year-old son at home and was about to deliver my daughter. I had no prospects of a job, and I'd just signed a contract to join this group practice and pay rent every month but had no idea how to build a practice.

I was glad I was in a closed door room with plenty of tissues because it truly felt like the opportune time and place to bawl my eyes out!

I went home that night and collapsed on my couch in defeat. Was I really up to this challenge? Where should I even begin? Who would teach me how to do this?

Over time, I started to learn how things worked. I asked therapists who worked at the group how they built their caseloads, how they set up their businesses, and how they got referrals. I told everyone who worked there that I was open to any client they couldn't take on and I was open to low-fee, sliding scale clients too while I was building up my hours toward licensure. I asked my supervisor more questions about business building than actual case consultation, but it's all I wanted to learn at the time.

I had a deep desire to help my future clients and never let go of my private practice vision.

I really admired one of the seasoned clinicians who worked at our group practice. Her name was Ann. She was a fully licensed PhD psychologist in the twilight of her career as a therapist, and her office always felt so inviting, smart, and safe to me. Like I could plop down on her big sectional and spill my guts to her, which is partly why she'd had such a long run as a successful clinician. Everything about her presence and her office felt like the quintessential world of therapy to me.

I explained my dilemma to her, and she could feel my eagerness to learn how to build a business of my own, so she agreed to take me under her wing and decided to run a little workshop for new therapists called "The Business of Doing Business." It was perfect! She gave me all the bits and pieces I needed to get established, like how to get my LLC and EIN, how to open a business bank account, how to do simple bookkeeping, as well as the ins and outs of effective marketing and referral network building.

I felt immediate relief.

I had guidance and a clear path. Ann gave me the keys to unlock my future, and it's all I needed to get started on my journey toward building a thriving practice.

Whether you're dreaming of building a practice or you've already built one and you're ready to scale your business, I'm sure you can relate to this feeling of excitement and terror all at once. Grad school gives us a lot of exceptional knowledge, but most programs leave a giant void in the business building side of private practice work. And because at the time of this publication, Continuing Education (CEs) cannot cover coaching, business building, marketing, or practice management topics, it becomes challenging for therapists to secure the knowledge they need to thrive.

I suppose the feeling of being so lost and confused, so disillusioned by the future of my own career path, left such a strong imprint on me that it motivates me daily to help support other therapists to feel confident and clear on building their own career trajectory. Coupled with my own history of trauma and uncertainty growing up around a father with chronic, pervasive mental health issues, my mission is twofold: to increase access to outpatient mental health care and to protect the therapists who serve those clients by helping them prevent burnout, increase their earning potential, and keep them thriving as therapists.

How Will This Book Help You Thrive?

Whether you're just finishing grad school or you're a late-career therapist looking to make a pivot with your business goals, the information here will help you thrive as a therapist.

You might want to build a private practice or you might feel ready to scale your business and take your work to the next level. Either way, this book is designed to help you save time and energy and fast-track your way to thriving as a therapist.

The material in this book is divided into three main sections. I invite you to take your time moving through this book. Take notes, pause to reflect, and use the information here to help you bring your vision of thriving to life!

The three sections include

- Building
- Scaling
- Thriving

First, an overview of how to build a thriving practice, which will cover the ins and outs of business building, marketing, building your online presence and referral network, setting your fees, defining your niche, making sure your caseload is full, and establishing your expertise and authority as a private practice owner. Even if you've built a thriving practice, you will still want to review this section. In this first section, you will discover new ideas and tips on authority building strategies, networking solutions you may have never thought of, and even money mindset shifts that will help you in other areas of business management and growth.

Second, we will move on to scaling your business, which involves lots of strategies to help you move beyond the 1:1 model of care. These concepts will help you increase your impact and your income. Once you fill your caseload to capacity, you essentially hit a glass ceiling of earning potential, and if you take on too many weekly clients to increase your income, you will quickly find yourself feeling burned out. I know this because I had a caseload of thirty-five clients every single week for ten years! Seven clients a day, five days a week, back to back without even taking a lunch break. I made the most money I possibly could in those ten years almost exclusively from private practice work, but I paid a serious price for it.

I was so tapped out from my clinical caseload and the intensity of that much direct care, I barely had room to interact with my family and friends. My downtime looked more like comfort care rather than replenishing and nourishing self-care. My quality of life suffered, and I noticed a sharp decline in my own sense of personal joy.

I wasn't thriving; I was barely surviving!

I knew something needed to change, so I started to consider how to make a shift and how to scale my business as a therapist. In section 2, I will cover how to increase your income and your impact by learning how to build group therapy groups, build retreats, create online courses, hire your first clinician, and build a group practice. I will also discuss how to build a coaching arm of your business, how to build a speaking career and secure paid talks, and how to build a platform or following and why this is so important. I'll review Facebook group building and how to nurture your email list, and I'll also cover outsourcing and how and when to hire support as you scale and level up your business.

And finally in section 2 of this book, you'll find out how to thrive as a therapist in your personal life. In this section, I'll cover the elusive work-life balance matrix and cover boundary management, self-care solutions that work, how and why we need to tap into our intuition as business owners, the importance of following your joy, connecting to your own authentic voice and value system as a business owner, and how to sustain your mission and purpose so you can enjoy a long thriving career as a therapist without burning out, becoming callous, or feeling disconnected from the work.

I'm on a mission to help therapists thrive in all aspects of their lives from personal to professional to financial. I'm also here to help you think and dream bigger and learn all the ways you can build a thriving career without burning out. There are many ways we can package up our knowledge and expertise and lots of ways we can serve clients in need of our support. Many therapists have been taught or told that "you can't make money in this field" or "social workers and counselors shouldn't charge that much" or "being a therapist means working all nights and weekends and it's super draining and exhausting work."

People actually said these things to me! But it doesn't have to be this way, and I'm here to show you how you can build a thriving life as a successful entrepreneur and enjoy prosperity, freedom, and joy!

What are you waiting for? Let's get started!

CHAPTER 1
Setting Up Your Business

So you made it through grad school—now what?!

Most graduate degrees for therapists spend very little time helping you understand how to set up a business. There's a lot to know when you build a business from scratch. Let's start with the basics.

Before you decide to build a practice, it's a good idea to get clear on your *why*. Why do you want to build a practice? Who do you want to serve? How will having a private practice help your clients, how will it help you, and how will it help your career development? There are a few basic steps you need to move through in order to set up your business correctly.

Disclaimer: None of the information in this chapter should replace professional consultation with your attorney or tax accountant. It's meant to give you some guideposts to follow, but some of these topics vary based on where you're building your practice and what the laws are in your area.

Step 1: Naming Your Business

This process takes a lot of time, clever thinking skills, and tons of patience. I recommend you do not name your business after your actual first and last name. I did this when I first started, grabbed the domain name www.megangunnell.com, filed my PLLC as Megan Gunnell, LMSW, PLLC, and opened a business bank account under my name and credentials too.

If you've already done this, don't worry. It's OK! But I want you, as a thriving therapist, to always think about your future vision. Someday this might be a sellable asset. You might grow your business and expand by hiring other therapists to join your practice and build a group practice. You might include trainings, workshops, or retreats down the road, and if you build your business to a substantial level of growth and earning potential, it could be something you sell one day.

But no one out there is going to buy "megangunnell.com," and no one would take over Megan Gunnell's solo private practice. That isn't a sellable asset. It's essentially my personal brand. And as I've grown over the years and added multiple streams of income, built a substantial platform, and added various additional companies to my portfolio as an entrepreneur, the fact that I have this domain and business name is something I use to essentially funnel people to the right arms of my multiple businesses. However, if I were to start all over again, I would certainly purchase and secure the domain that was my first and last name, but I would build my practice under a business name that could be purchased by someone else down the road if I decided to scale and sell that business in the future.

Think of a name that is also not location specific. There's nothing worse than building an entire company and brand awareness around your city, and then finding out that you need to relocate. And remember, your business could be a multi-state or a national business one day too. So you wouldn't want to call it the "Chicago Counseling Center" or something like that if you end up serving clients across many states or across the country in your future.

You also want to be sure that your name is original and doesn't spell anything strange if you break it down to just an acronym. In order to make sure you've chosen an original business name, be sure to google it, check sites like GoDaddy.com, and do a deep search across all social media platforms to be sure that you haven't just landed on a name that someone else has perhaps put a trademark on already.

When you select your business name, try to get the exact same domain name in a .com format. Avoid periods or hyphens in your domain name, and once you land on the perfect business name, I recommend that you purchase the .com, .net, and .org versions of your domain in addition to securing all of the social media handles for this name too, even if you're not ready to use all of them yet.

If you're having trouble coming up with a business name, try to brain dump every single word that represents what you do for your clients, or what you hope you will do or provide to them in sessions. What really represents the mood, tone, and feeling of what you do as a business owner and psychotherapist? How would others describe what you do and how you work? What mission or vision do you have for your company? How does that tie into what you're offering to your clients?

When you come up with a word or phrase that you absolutely love, check to make sure it's available. If it's not available, consider adding a word to your business name such as center, institute, collective, or something else that represents what you could grow into.

Once you've named your business, you're ready for step 2.

Step 2: Form Your Business Structure Such as an LLC or PLLC

The next step is to register your business as a formal business entity. Most people form an LLC or PLLC. In some states, they make you do this through an attorney, but most states allow you to file this paperwork yourself. You can speak to your accountant or tax advisor as to what makes more sense for your business. As your business grows and you are comfortably making a more significant profit, it might make sense to form an S corp. Your accountant can guide you on the pros and cons of these business decisions based on your revenue, expenses, and other factors.

Once you have filed this and it's been approved, you're ready for step 3.

Step 3: Apply for an EIN with the IRS

Next, go to IRS.gov and apply for your EIN. This is your employee identification number that you will use in place of your SSN on all business-related documents and for tax purposes. You cannot apply for this until you've completed the step above this. Having an EIN protects you from using your SSN on your business documents, and forming your business in this way also protects you. It helps you separate your personal assets from your business assets too.

PRO TIP: As soon as they send you the paperwork that says what your EIN is, be sure to make a copy of this and maybe email it to yourself and then file the original in a very safe place. You sometimes need to show proof of this original EIN document, and if you lose it, it is very difficult and time-consuming to replace.

Step 4: Liability Insurance

Be sure to secure the appropriate amount of liability insurance for your practice. There are many companies that offer plans for psychotherapists, so be sure to shop around for the best coverage and best pricing. You will want to be sure to get a plan that offers at a minimum $1,000,000 per claim insuring agreement and $3,000,000 aggregate. If you're offering telehealth sessions, you will need to add some type of cyber coverage in addition to your regular coverage. As your practice expands, if you hire therapists to join your team and form a group practice, you'll also need to notify your insurance provider so they can adjust your plan accordingly and cover each new therapist under your group practice.

Step 5: Taking Insurance

If you want to take insurance and get credentialed with health insurance companies, you'll need to file for a National Provider Identifier (NPI) number and complete a Council for Affordable Quality Healthcare (CAQH) profile. This section could be an entire second book! Instead of adding all of that information here, I highly recommend you connect with experts who specialize in billing and insurance such as Kym Tolson or Gabrielle Juliano-Villani.

Step 6: Business Banking

Once you have your business structure set up and your EIN established, you're ready to open a business bank account. I always recommend setting this up at a national bank rather than a small local credit union. As your business expands, you will want the perks that large banks provide to you, and changing your business bank accounts later can be a tedious process. That said, I also recommend that you read the fine print and fully understand the requirements of the accounts that you open such as minimum balances you must maintain to avoid penalties, as well as any fees or charges for any account you open.

I recommend that you set up a business checking account and two business savings accounts. One of your savings accounts will be used for setting aside your quarterly estimated tax percentage. I recommend moving 25–30 percent of every payment you receive over to this savings account. Then when it's time to pay your quarterly taxes, you have enough saved for these payments ahead of time. The second savings account should be used for general business savings. Put whatever you can into this account on a regular basis. Then when it's time to make business purchases, you'll have a savings account with money earmarked for these expenditures.

It's also a good idea to apply for a business credit card, but you may need to do this after showing you have business income over a certain period of time. You can pay yourself by doing what's called an "owner's draw" where you transfer money from your business to personal accounts or cut yourself a check. If one day you expand into forming an S corp, then you will put yourself on the payroll as a W2 employee and pay yourself a paycheck from your company. But, until you do that, you can simply pay yourself weekly or twice a month from your business checking account.

Be sure to consult with an accountant who specializes in small businesses. They will help you identify business expenses and deductions and help you know how much to set aside and pay for your estimated quarterly federal and state taxes.

If you're looking for more help with this, I recommend checking out Jennie Schottmiller of Simple Profit.

Step 7: Set Up Your Business to Receive Payments

How will clients pay you? You can set up a business Square account, use companies like Ivy Pay, or build a business electronic health record

(EHR) system for your practice on platforms such as Owl Practice, SimplePractice, or TherapyNotes where clients will be charged for cash fee sessions, copays, or deductible charges right inside your platform. That money typically moves from the software platform to a company like Stripe and then to your business bank account. It's very simple to use and helps make payment collection easy for you and your clients.

I recommend steering clear of using PayPal or Venmo for your business payment transactions. You would never use PayPal or Venmo to pay your doctor, dentist, or lawyer. Using these platforms suggests a less than professional practice management system to your clients and can decrease trust in you as the clinician and business owner of your practice.

Step 8: Setting Up Your Office

Will you have a brick-and-mortar office for in-person visits, or will you practice virtually as a telehealth provider or maybe a hybrid model where you have a mix of both offerings?

If you're searching for office space, you will want to consider the following: parking, accessibility, noise/soundproofing, security, who cleans the common areas, insurance for your space, bathroom accessibility, kitchenette access, space for 1:1 work as well as group therapy or small meeting space, temperature control, windows, who pays for electricity, water, gas, etc.?

Negotiating a lease is something you should take your time with. Try to find out whether you can speak to previous tenants that this landlord has worked with. This will give you a lot of info on whether or not they had a good experience renting in that office building or not.

Also be sure to find out how much the rent will increase from contract to contract. One year I went to renew my lease and discovered my landlord had increased my rent by 25 percent, which was absolutely unheard of in my area. This should not be allowed and is something to be cautious about right from the start.

If you're working from home for telehealth sessions, you'll want to consider the following factors: having strong Wi-Fi, having a private and confidential space to work from (that is ideally not your bedroom), having a platform for video sessions that is confidential, secure, and HIPAA compliant.

You will also need to have a business address for your work, even if you are 100 percent virtual. You can use your home address or a virtual business address.

In the next few chapters, we will dive into developing a marketing plan and building your referral network so you can keep your caseload full!

CHAPTER 2
Marketing Your Practice

Buckle your seat belts and get your highlighters ready! This chapter is going to help you define your practice and keep your caseload full.

We are highly skilled clinicians, but many of us fall short in the marketing "know-how" department. But don't worry. In this chapter, we will cover the most fundamental marketing elements that will help your practice thrive.

Establish and Define Your Niche

Spend some time considering your niche or preferred area of focus for your practice. Even if you're just starting out, you might be able to narrow this down by considering areas of interest to you in grad school or in your internship or practicum training. You may also know what areas you do not want to focus on (maybe couples therapy or working with kids or teens, for example). You might also prefer working with a certain population or diagnosis such as women with anxiety or postpartum depression, or maybe addiction work interests you.

There are no right or wrong answers here. Give yourself an opportunity to brainstorm.

Do you envision that your practice will offer more wellness or holistic care? Maybe incorporating other modalities such as yoga or meditation? Or will you offer testing for clients around a certain diagnosis or specialty? Do you see yourself being an expert in trauma and using Eye Movement

Desensitization and Reprocessing (EMDR), for example?

What direction are you leaning toward? Who is your ideal client? Spend a little time considering your perfect client and everything you might imagine about them.

Once you get a good idea of who this ideal client might be, it will help you build your marketing materials to attract them to your practice. Next, you'll want to spend some time thinking about what problems your ideal client might have and what results they might be looking for as they enter a therapeutic relationship with you.

Spend a few moments answering these questions now before moving on to the next section.

Your Online Presence

Most potential clients are finding out about you in two ways: from a Google search or from a referral source. Let's be sure that the Google search helps them find their way to you and that when they find you, they understand immediately that you're the best person to help them with their needs right now.

Remember that anything you're building in an online space is answering the questions and concerns that your ideal client might have. If you can frame your practice information how your ideal client might be thinking and feeling, they will read what's on your website or online profile account and instantly feel like you understand them and what they need before they even reach out to schedule with you.

In order to speak to your potential client in a way that helps them feel as if you're speaking directly to them, ask questions in your opening statements on your directory profile (i.e., Psychology Today) or in the top fold of your website. Open with something you think they might be experiencing such as "Do you toss and turn at night because you have so many thoughts running through your mind?" or "Do you feel misunderstood in your relationship or that your partner just doesn't hear what you're trying to convey?" The more specific you are, the better your client conversion rates will be.

You only have ten seconds to help your ideal client believe that you're the right therapist for them before they back out of your site and go on to search for the next therapist. Be sure that your first three sentences help them know they're in the right place.

You do this by making sure that you start by addressing them and their concerns first, not by talking about yourself and your expertise, training, or education. They can always go deeper to find out where you got your degree or which certifications you hold, your work experience, or what you specialize in, but if you instantly connect to how they might be feeling when they're searching for a therapist, it's more probable that they will reach out to schedule with you. If you quickly establish your authority and expertise and you have a clear call to action step for the potential client to connect with you and schedule a session, it's more likely that they will convert to working with you and another therapist/client match will be made.

It's a good idea to have a profile on directory sites like TherapyDen or Psychology Today, but it's even better if you're able to make a website too. Even a simple contact funnel website helps legitimize your practice and demonstrate your expertise.

Think about your personal life. When you want to try out a new doctor or new restaurant or even want to book a hotel room, think about what you do. You google it. You like to legitimize the person, the service, or the place you're going, and viewing a website helps you make that determination. On some occasions, places are so highly recommended to you that you don't care whether they have a website or not because you've heard they're so amazing, you're willing to trust that word-of-mouth referral and overlook the fact that they do not have any "online real estate." This could be true also for your practice. I know therapists who built very successful careers and never had a website, but they also had a thriving referral network and a highly defined niche that they specialized in serving.

In general, it's a good idea for marketing purposes to control the narrative of who you are, who you serve, and how people can reach you, and you can do that easily by building a simple website.

What to Include on Your Website?

At the very least, you will need a header, footer, professional photos of yourself, and these four pages:

1. Home
2. About
3. Services
4. Contact Us

Each page should have clear call to action buttons that guide the user to connect with you or find out more information.

Your home page is an overview of who you serve and how you help them with links that go to your about, services, and contact pages.

Your about page is where you can really share all of the relevant info on why you're an amazing therapist! Don't be afraid to let your bio shine. This is your chance to brag a bit about your education and training, additional certifications, awards, publications, and anything extra like any podcasts you've been a guest on, for example, or any media attention of you or your work.

Your about page should also have really professional photos of you that are clear, in focus, and immediately give a sense of your personality and style. It's also nice to sometimes include a sentence at the end of your about page that talks about what you like doing in your free time. Be clever and descriptive with the language on your about page. It should invite the reader to know more about who you are as a therapist and a person and what you believe in too.

Your services page can include information like your hours of operation, your fees, and which insurances you accept. You can also include how you practice (i.e., in person or virtual or both), as well as how you treat clients (which modalities you use such as EMDR, CBT, DBT, etc.). This page can also include information about the Good Faith Estimate and any other information you want to include about the logistics and details of how you serve your clients.

Your contact page is a simple contact funnel that allows clients to email, call, or even directly schedule with you depending on what you prefer. You might also include a map of your location if you have a physical office.

Ideally, a website would also include a blog, press page, and maybe even a recommended resources page too. Your press page comes in handy if you're pitching to speak at conferences or you start to get quoted in articles. Then you can send people directly to a page on your website that has high-resolution downloadable photos, links to all of your social media accounts, and a list of everywhere you've presented or been quoted or interviewed, all in one place.

As your practice and business grows, you can add specialty pages like a speaking page or a page for your online courses or retreats. We'll dive into those ideas a lot more in section 2 of this book.

Blogs are a fantastic way to build better SEO (search engine optimization) for your practice, and they're also a good way for prospective clients to get a better understanding of you and the way you practice. Blogs can be evergreen content, your original thoughts on a topic, a guest expert interview (great for cross-promoting with a colleague or referral source), or they can even be a review of a new book, podcast, or form of treatment that you think your clients should know about. When you post a new blog, remember to share it and repurpose it several times. You can send it out in your client newsletter and post it to all of your social media sites and your LinkedIn profile.

When I was blogging on a regular basis for about three years, my website was always the first therapist's website that popped up in my zip code when people searched for "therapist near me." My blog also gave me an instant authority boost when I was being considered for speaking gigs or quotes in other larger publications.

When using stock images for your blog posts or anywhere else on your website, be sure to search for copyright-free images on sites such as Unsplash.com rather than simply selecting an image you googled that may not be copyright-free. You can face steep fines if you use a copyrighted image without permission.

But for the best SEO results, it's better to use your own images rather than stock images. So remember this when you have professional photos done and get a lot of lifestyle and branding images in addition to the traditional head and shoulders, smile and shoot headshots. It's also helpful to have several inbound links from other reputable sites (like Psychology Today) going to your site.

Social Media Tips

First rule: **Never** friend or follow clients or allow clients to friend or follow you on your personal social media pages. It's unethical, unprofessional, and a breach of privacy and confidentiality. It can negatively impact how you build trust in your therapeutic relationship with your client.

Instead, set up business social media pages. Consider LinkedIn for all of your networking and professional contacts and business accounts on Facebook, Instagram, YouTube, or TikTok for your business marketing.

Just choose one or two platforms to focus on. You do not need to be an expert on every single social media platform. Where would you get the biggest bang for your buck? I recommend having a LinkedIn page for your professional networking (referral sources, speaking offers, collaborations with colleagues, interviews to be a guest on podcasts, etc.). And then choose either a business Facebook and/or Instagram page to focus on where clients can follow you, learn more about you and how you work, reach out to schedule with you, and share your info with other prospective clients.

Be sure to complete all the basic info in each social media profile and use your company name, business name, credentials, business website, business work address, phone, website, and email contacts. Consider using the same headshot or logo for the profile pic or thumbnail image for brand recognition throughout all of your offerings.

Share valuable content with your audience and mix up your posts with articles, research, quick tips, personal reflections, inspirational quotes or messages, and info about your offerings. You don't want your social media pages to only be announcements about things you published or only things you're offering, otherwise people will become turned off or disengaged, or they will hide you if it feels too salesy. You want posts that create high engagement. You want to keep your client in mind when sharing things on these pages. Share questions that invite people to give answers in long comments or prompt them to dialog with each other.

Remember, when it comes to social media, you're creating a community, a conversation, and you want your page to be a resource. It shouldn't be just a constant stream of marketing ads running to your practice website. It should be engaging and valuable to anyone who follows your pages.

Building a Platform

It's a good idea to begin building your platform or audience as you build your practice. A simple way to do this is to ask for permission to add a new client's email to your mailing list on your intake form. Choose an email service provider and begin entering client emails as you get them. As you begin to scale and grow, you'll have an audience of clients to share your blog posts with and your workshop or retreat offerings, etc. You might find that they begin sharing your valuable blog or video content with people in their circles too, and that's how your clients refer you to others and help you build a thriving practice. We will go into a lot more detail on platform building as we scale our businesses in section 2.

Printed Marketing Materials

All you need to get started with printed marketing materials is a business card and a rack card.

You can make business cards and rack cards easily on sites like Vistaprint.

Your business cards should

- Look professional
- Have a logo
- Clearly display your name, credentials, title, and phone number
- Include your email, website, and social media info

Remember your branding (color scheme, font, logo, tagline) can all be represented in a uniform way from business card to rack card to website to social media pages. You're establishing a brand identity by keeping everything uniform across all of your marketing channels.

Your rack cards should look professional and have all of the same info as your business card, but they also can include the following:
- A professional headshot
- A short bulleted list of your areas of expertise (specializing in treating anxiety, depression, mood disorders, etc.)
- A short bio
- A quote or your tagline for your company and brand

Do not put too much info on a rack card—you want someone to be able to glance at it and see immediately what it is you offer and understand the messaging.

Once you create rack cards, send them all over and hand-deliver them with the plastic holders to your referral sources. Think doctors' offices, psychiatrist offices, pediatricians, school counseling offices, funeral homes, etc. And keep a record of your referral sources. Note the name of your referral source, their location, when you stopped by or reached out, and what action you took; for example, emailed about taking new insurances, or dropped off rack cards. This will help you remember when to reach out again and what steps to take next time you connect with your referral source.

Psychology Today or Other Online Directories: Why Some Therapists Get All the Referrals

The best way to get a lot of traffic on Psychology Today is to have a professional headshot and a great opening paragraph that captures what your potential client is thinking and feeling. You also want to be very specific about your area of expertise. Many times referral sources at hospitals or other medical offices search Psychology Today for referrals. If they see you specialize in all ages and all areas of need, they'll move along to the next profile. Be specific. You can't treat everyone. Only select the issues you treat that are truly in your area of expertise. You do not want to look like a generalist. You want to make it clear that you have an area of expertise.

I've seen therapists list that they treat ages zero through one hundred. That would be a red flag for me if I were a client looking for an expert. Narrow down your niche and remember to connect your website to your profile. Having outbound links from larger websites to your website helps your SEO too.

Psychology Today Profile Quick Tips

- Use a professional, warm, friendly headshot.
- Start your description with questions your ideal client might resonate with.
- Niche down! Do not look like a generalist. Be very specific about what ages you serve and what issues you treat.
- Do include your price range and which insurances you take.
- Tweak and change your profile from time to time. A refreshed profile will remain closer to the top of the search in your zip code vs. a profile that has not been altered or changed in any way for a long time.
- Include extra photos of yourself (professional shots) or photos of your office space.
- Link your website to your profile.
- Be sure to include your professional license number.
- Ask colleagues for endorsements.
- Add any groups you might be offering too.

Letters to Your Referral Sources

A referral letter is also a great idea. Print it in color with your letterhead at the top on high-quality paper. Keep it short and succinct. Introduce yourself, featuring your title, expertise, and background. Make it known that you are accepting new referrals and whether or not you accept insurance. Use a bullet list to feature what conditions you treat and include business cards or rack cards with your letter. Remember to address the mutual benefit of your referral relationship and follow up after you mail it to see whether you can secure a call or in-person meeting to discuss how your business can support their clients, patients, or customers.

Use Your Existing Network and Think Outside the Box

Tell everyone you're a therapist! The more you self-identify, the more the world will recognize you as such. Share info about your practice online and with your personal and professional network.

Think beyond doctors, lawyers, funeral directors, hospital social workers, and school counselors. Many therapists do very well filling their caseload by networking with other therapists with similar specialities who may be at capacity and need a referral source for overflow clients. You can also make your practice information known to therapists who have a specialty that is very different from yours. Some therapists are seeking trusted referral sources for specialities they do not provide. You can reach out directly to therapists in your area by finding them on Psychology Today, LinkedIn, local therapist Facebook groups, and even the local chamber of commerce.

Your best referral sources might be people you already know like your dentist, hairdresser, or yoga instructor. Clients are sometimes searching for support from their own trusted network of business owners or practitioners. Make it known that you are open to new referrals with anyone in your circle of business too. You just never know where your next referral might come from.

You can also pitch to write an article for the local paper, like a "Dear Abby" or advice column where you provide your own hypothetical client question and then answer it as the expert.

Or perhaps your community is experiencing something collectively? Like collective grief or circumstantial depression or anxiety (potentially due to economic, climate, or occupational challenges that are specific to your location). As a therapist, you could provide an op-ed or pitch an article to the paper suggesting coping strategies, resources for readers to get more help, or warning signs when symptoms need treatment or support. Editors are searching for valuable content each week. There is no harm in emailing your local paper to find out whether they might accept an article from you. Your byline would identify you as a local expert and include your website where readers could go for more support.

Offer Presentations

Reach out to local support groups, clubs, associations, and organizations and offer yourself as a speaker. Mention what your expertise is, share a link to your website, and tell them why you think their audience would benefit from your presentation. Clubs and groups are always searching for speakers. Offer a presentation to your local library. Once you do several presentations for free, you'll be able to build upon that and expand into paid offers. You can add a speaking page to your website and add photos and video clips of your recent talks.

You can also google "call for proposals _____ conferences" and find current listings for conferences that are accepting pitches for breakout and keynote speakers. You can submit to be a speaker at a local conference and use that network to expand your referral resources!

Providing Excellent Service

What's your #1 way to get the most new referrals and keep your practice thriving? Provide the very best care possible to your current clients. Treat them with the utmost respect and dignity. Run sessions on time and stay present and connected to each client you work with.

Take good notes and review them carefully before each session to be sure that you're clear on where you left off at the last session and clear on what goals you're working toward.

Maintain best practices. Stay current on what the best treatment options are for your area of expertise and for your clients' needs. Know your referral sources well (for medication management options and other recommended experts that might be beneficial to your clients' course of treatment).

When we provide excellent service to our clients, our clients sing our praises and refer our services to others and/or return to their referral source and thank them, which in turn will build confidence in your referral sources to continue sending new clients to your practice.

Online Presence Checklist

Check these tasks off as you complete them.

- ☐ Google yourself—what do you notice? Check Google Images too. Make sure your online presence reflects what you want the world to see or know about you.

- ☐ Be sure that everything you share online reflects the professional that you are (think social media profile pics, social media posts, LinkedIn profile, etc.). If a client googles you, will they see something you wouldn't want them to see?

- ☐ If a client lands on your information in a search to find a therapist, will they resonate with your messaging within ten to twenty seconds? You should be answering questions *they* have first, then sharing about your expertise second. Will they immediately resonate with the questions you're posting on your website or on your Psychology Today profile?

- ☐ Does your website have clear calls to action? Each page of your site should have a clear call to action. For example, at the end of a page after they scroll down, there should be a simple way for them to connect with you—a button to push to email you, an embedded phone number so they can click and call you, or a scheduling app where they can select an appointment time themselves. Another option would be to have a button that links them to another section of your website such as your blog page, press page, about me page, etc.

CHAPTER 3

Building Your Referral Network

As therapists, we're in the business of human relationships. It makes sense then, that one of the most beneficial ways we can fill our caseload is by building really solid referral relationships and a robust referral network. Doing this correctly is more than simply sending some business cards to a doctor who you think might want to refer to you. It goes well beyond a one-time point of contact. What you want to do is foster a mutually beneficial, solid referral network of professionals who will think of you first when the need comes up for psychotherapy services.

First, let's begin by considering all the people who might be the very best referral sources for you and your practice specialties. For my own practice, I focused a lot on women's health. I addressed depression, anxiety, life transitions, and grief and loss so naturally the best referral sources for me were ob-gyns.

When I was first starting out, I sent out three hundred letters to ob-gyns in a tri-county area. I thought, *This is it! As soon as these doctors get my info, my practice will be booming and my caseload will be full.*

I remember stuffing all of the letters with some of my business cards, addressing and licking the envelopes, adding stamps to them, and dropping them in the mail. I thought that in less than a week, the phone would be ringing off the hook.

I was wrong!

It was total crickets. Most of the doctors who received my letter probably tossed it in the trash either before they opened it or as soon as they read what was inside. I was asking *them* to help *me*. I didn't have anything in the letter that addressed how I could help make their work easier. Only one doctor called me back, and it was because he was also brand new to that area. He called me to set up an appointment time for me to go visit him in his office and talk a little about my services.

I was so excited! My first real referral source!

During our conversation, a light bulb went off for me. I realized suddenly that the only reason he'd asked me to come in was that he wanted me to refer to him. Yes, of course he was hearing me talk about my services too, but he really wanted to be sure I knew all about his brand-new office and what services he could provide to my clients.

This was my intro to the world of building mutually beneficial relationships with your referral sources. In order for a busy referral source to make time to meet with you, they're going to want to know what's in it for them. Once I learned this, I changed the way I approached new referral sources. I thought about how many ob-gyns feel rushed to see a lot of patients in one day and how many of those patients likely are dealing with depression, anxiety, life transitions, and grief and loss and how the doctors do not have time to address the mental health issues that show up during a physical exam.

From then on, I structured my letters to address the problem areas and pain points of my referral sources (much like we structure our online marketing, websites, and Psychology Today profiles to address the problems and pain points of our ideal clients).

Once I started doing this, I built stronger, more effective relationships with my referral sources. They felt like I was an asset to their work. That I could assist them in making their jobs easier and faster by referring their patients out to me and my practice for the mental health needs of their patients.

It's critical that you don't stop here.

Once you form a referral relationship, you want to nurture it. You want to support their business social media pages, like their posts, connect with them on LinkedIn, invite them to be a guest expert on your podcast or blog or interview them for a guest expert interview video for your practice, and cross-promote their info across your online spaces and ask them to do the same for you too.

When you see opportunities such as a call for speakers or a HARO (Help a Reporter Out) query that might be beneficial for them to answer, shoot them an email and send it their way. When you show your referral sources that you're interested in this type of collaboration and support, it helps you form a stronger working partnership with them.

On your client intake form, insert a line that says "Referred by:_____ May we thank them? _____" If your client lists who they were referred by and agrees to allow you to thank them, you can send that referral source a personal note with more business cards inside to help them keep you and your practice top of mind when referring out. You do not need to identify anything about the client who was referred.

You can simply say

Dear Dr. _____,

Thank you for your recent referral. I met with your patient for an initial intake visit (today, yesterday, last week), and I look forward to providing support and (strategies for symptom management, coping, etc.).

As always, I cannot thank you enough for your trust and confidence in my services. I've enclosed a few extra business cards and welcome future referrals. It's a pleasure to support your patients.

When forming brand-new referral relationships, send your info to them in a personalized letter. Offer value to their clients/patients/students/support group members. Consider the benefit you bring to them or their services (via referrals back to them, a complimentary presentation, lunch and learn, virtual or in-person offerings, etc.). Think for a moment about what you could include. Who are you reaching out to, what value are you bringing to them, what's your call to action? Could you create a valuable handout for your referral source?

What's a question they get all the time in their office that you can help answer as a mental health professional? Could you build a valuable resource list on your website and make your referral source aware of that? There are lots of ways to do this; you just have to remember to bring high value to the referral source and the population they serve.

It's also a good idea to consider any crossover with your referral network. Where can you overlap your areas of expertise? A local event, media spot, conference, or opportunity to present somewhere together? The opportunities are truly endless.

Another way you can leverage your referral relationships is by asking them for endorsements or testimonials you can share on your website or online directory like your Psychology Today profile. Since we cannot get testimonials from clients, it's a good idea to build that level of social proof by asking your trusted referral sources for one. Of course, you will need to have established a good track record of excellent service to their population, but over time as you build this, you can ask them for a two- to three-sentence testimonial or endorsement to help you build that layer of trust across your online real estate.

Lastly, take a moment now and list ten people in your circle of contacts who might benefit from knowing more about the services you provide:

1. _____

2. _____

3. _____

4. _____

5. _____

6. _____

7. _____

8. _____

9. _____

10. _____

Get your info in front of these contacts ASAP! Email them, send or drop off business cards or rack cards, message them on social media, make a connection and follow up.

CHAPTER 4

Practice Management—Setting Your Fees, Setting Up Your Policies

Once you've set up the bones to your business, you've designed your marketing strategy, and you've started to build your referral network, you're ready to see clients! Starting your own outpatient practice is daunting. Even if you've had tons of training and experience working with clients in other settings, there's nothing that prepares you for sitting face-to-face with your first client in private practice. It's a strange feeling. You're completely in charge. The client is looking to you to direct everything, and yet they're typically feeling eager and scared to get started too.

Since this chapter is all about practice management skills, let's start at the very beginning—the client's inquiry to you. Typically clients will email or call you to inquire whether you're accepting new clients. It's really important to try to respond to them as soon as you are able. Many times clients are reaching out to multiple providers, and I found the faster I was able to connect with them, the more likely they would schedule with me.

Things to Cover in the First Point of Contact

Whether you're calling or emailing the client back, it's a good idea to try to find out a few important pieces of information. First, do they want to use their insurance or will this be a private pay client? If they want to use their insurance and you do not accept it, you have a couple of options. You can find out more about why they're scheduling with you, describe your expertise in that area, and discuss your cash fee rates. You can offer a superbill if you are able to provide this to your clients. A superbill is like a specialty receipt for a cash fee session that the client uses to submit to their insurance company for partial or full reimbursement under their out-of-network benefits (if they have these under their plan). In order to provide a superbill to clients, you must have an NPI number and a tax ID number, and you must include the client's date of birth, address, name, diagnosis code, date of session, amount charged, and the CPT or service code for your session (such as the 90791 or 90837).

Once you find out more about whether they want to use their insurance or will be a private pay client and pay your cash fee rate, you can offer three to four session times that work for your schedule so they can choose their intake appointment time. Build your schedule thoughtfully. Do not ask the client when they want to be seen, but rather decide what your preferred hours will be and build your sessions around other scheduled sessions. If someone is already booked at 11 a.m. on your calendar, then offer your new client the slot before and the slot after that scheduled session.

As you go to reschedule clients, you can discuss whether they want to have a standing appointment time with you or pick from three to four options again. Each time you offer those session times, just be sure that they are truly at times you are fully available and wanting to schedule. There's nothing worse than bending to accommodate a client's request for a time that is not a preferred slot for you, and then you find yourself feeling burdened or resentful about having to show up for that session. And even worse, if the client forgets, no-shows, or needs to reschedule, this can really create frustration for you as the provider and that frustration can negatively impact the therapeutic relationship.

You will need to get your clients' info and make sure they review and complete all of your new client paperwork (intake forms, informed consent, privacy policies) and submit their insurance info and payment information. EHR software systems such as Owl Practice, SimplePractice, or TherapyNotes make this easy! They have forms and templates inside their system that you can use or adapt to your needs.

I always encourage new therapists to include the following questions on their intake form: "Who were you referred by?" and "May we thank them?" This way you can keep track of which referral sources are referring to you, and you can follow up with more business cards or rack cards as needed for those referral sources.

Another question you can add to your intake form is "May we add you to our newsletter/email list?" This way you can share your blog, podcast, practice updates, recommended resources, quick tips, and information with all of your clients in a simple and easy way. I wrote blog posts on a regular basis for my clinical solo practice for many years. I would email them to my clients about twice a month. Clients could unsubscribe from the email list at any time, but many appreciated the information I shared in my client newsletter, and in turn, views to my blog increased my SEO on my website too.

One last thought on this first step is even when your practice is at capacity, it's important that you call the client back and let them know. This is not only helpful for the client who's searching for a provider, but it's also a courtesy you should provide that will help maintain a reputation of "best practices" within your referral network and community. If a referral source who relies on you a lot heard back from a client they referred to you that you called them back promptly to let them know you were full and provided a few other referrals of providers in the area whom you trust that they could try to schedule with, it helps reinstill trust from that referral source back to you in the future when you have openings again in your caseload.

Setting Your Rates

Figuring out what to charge is one of the hardest parts of starting a practice for some therapists. A good rule of thumb is to see what the market will support in your location. Setting fees has a lot to do with location, expertise, niche and specialty, and years of experience in the field. Therapists in LA or NYC will likely be able to secure higher rates than therapists in rural communities. But that's not always the case. If you are a highly skilled, highly specialized, experienced provider, and there are very few who do what you do in your area, you can garner a higher fee than a therapist with less experience who's offering more generalized support (for depression and generalized anxiety, for example).

I remember asking other therapists in my group practice what to charge when I first started, and a very wise clinician said, "You'll be able to feel it intuitively if it's too high or too low."

There are practicalities to consider when establishing your rate such as figuring out what your overhead expenses are. Do you have to cover a brick-and-mortar monthly rent? How much are your other expenses such as your liability insurance, Wi-Fi, computer and phone expenses, your EHR platform costs, your marketing budget (Psychology Today profile or website fees), and any other expenses to consider when you're running your business?

Take the time to crunch the numbers.

Add up all of your business expenses and figure out what your monthly fees are to "keep your doors open." Then divide that number by the number of clients you'd like to see each month, keeping in mind that a full caseload is around twenty clients a week, not thirty-five like I was doing for way too many years. This will give you your "break-even" cost. But you're not a nonprofit. You want to make a good living being a therapist. And you deserve to make a good living in this field. You're highly skilled and you're literally saving lives.

Do not undervalue your role and expertise, even if you're brand new to the field.

I encourage you to do a little rate setting meditation exercise. I do this exercise anytime I'm setting fees for anything I'm doing as an entrepreneur such as 1:1 sessions, courses, coaching, retreats, workshops, speaking gigs, supervision—anything I'm charging for.

First, quiet your mind and remove all distractions for a few moments. Take a few cleansing breaths to feel grounded and in tune. Next, close your eyes and focus inward. Inside yourself, ask what your rate should be for your 1:1 session work. You might be surprised by the number that you feel, hear, or see in your mind's eye or from your intuitive knowing. It could be higher than you expected. But when you settle into that number for a moment, you will really feel inside yourself whether it is too high or too low.

The nice thing about being in private practice is you can adapt and change your rates at any time. If you find yourself feeling even one ounce of resentment toward your work, it could be that you're not charging enough or it could be that you've taken on too many clients or scheduled them at a time that is not ideal for your preferred schedule.

I remember when I was first building my practice, I was so eager to fill my caseload that I would book clients at any time slot that I felt would work best for them (mistake #1), and I accepted very low sliding scale rates when clients said they couldn't afford my regular cash fee rate (mistake #2). I had very young children when I was building my practice, and if my husband wasn't home, I had to arrange and pay for childcare so I could go to my office and work. Sometimes I had scheduled clients for evening appointments (the worst possible time for me mentally), and it required that I leave my children in the evening to go to my office to see these clients. If they were a sliding scale client and I was paying for childcare and they no-showed me, I was livid!

This was my first step in identifying how important professional boundaries are.

If we don't manage our professional boundaries with regard to our schedules, our rates, and what type of clients we are willing to take on or refer out, this work can easily upset or drain us. My goal is to help you have a long, healthy, prosperous, and thriving career as a therapist. I hope this book helps you avoid making the same mistakes I did.

Once you settle on your cash fee rate, the next step is to remember that you're telling people what it is, you're not asking for permission to charge that rate. If clients feel your rate is cost prohibitive to them, you can provide them with other more affordable options for therapy or offer a sliding scale.

It's also typical to charge more for your first one to two intake appointments and then charge your regular hourly session rate for your ongoing sessions.

How to Establish Your Sliding Scale Rate

It's best to establish what the lowest end of your sliding scale you're willing to offer is before you find yourself in a conversation with a client about your sliding scale rates. If your rate, for example, is $150/session and you're only comfortable going down to $90 a session, then that is perfectly acceptable. You're the boss and you get to decide what your rates are. Again, if they are too high for your client, there are many other options for care that you can help guide them to, or you could offer group sessions thereby allowing the client to access group therapy at a lower rate, but you're able to make more than you would in an individual hourly session.

It's OK to say to a client asking about your sliding scale that "I leave a few slots open for those going through a temporary economic hardship. My typical rate is X, but I'm willing to offer a sliding scale rate temporarily." This indicates that you only have a few sliding scale slots open at any given time and that the sliding scale is meant to be a temporary courtesy, not a rate that this client could have for the duration of their care with you unless of course you are OK with that.

This way, if a client is temporarily unemployed or going through a divorce, for example, and they anticipate alleviating those financial burdens within a few months' time, then they will be expected to move to your full session fee or use their insurance if you're in network with their new plan. Do not allow yourself to take on too many sliding scale clients, and be sure that you and the client feel comfortable with and clear on the parameters of what your sliding scale rate is and for how long you both might anticipate having it in place.

When I set up my sliding scale clients this way, it worked very well. I remember a client coming into her session after finding a new job and telling me with pride that she was ready to move to my full session fee, thereby opening up a sliding scale slot for someone else in need.

No-Shows and Late Cancellation Fees

Another thing that can be really difficult for new therapists is setting and adhering to your policies for no-shows and late cancellations. Your time and expertise are very valuable, and if a client happens to forget their session or cancels without enough notice, you have the right to charge them for that time that you cannot fill with another paying client.

It's a good idea to mention your policies to new clients three times before you actually begin working together. The first time is at the time of scheduling their intake. Whether on the phone or in an email, you will want to let them know that they need to give you twenty-four hours' notice (or whatever your policy is) if they need to cancel or reschedule for any reason. You will also want this listed in your paperwork that they review and sign. And I also always start every new client session by saying this:

> *"Before we begin, I would like to go over two quick practice policies with you. First, anything you share will remain confidential, unless there's an intent to hurt yourself or someone else. And second, I do require twenty-four hours' notice to cancel or make any changes to your appointment, otherwise you will be billed the full session fee."*

By this point, the client has heard about your no-show and late cancellation policy once at the time of scheduling, once in your practice paperwork, and once from you directly before you even begin the first session. When you make sure they understand your policy, then typically if they no-show or cancel without twenty-four hours' notice, they willingly offer up their accountability and acknowledge that there is a charge for this missed session.

Of course, as the practice owner, you can determine whether you want to have exceptions to this rule. I never charged if they were ill or had a sick child, or if they had an emergency, caregiver issues, or car trouble, for example. But, if they slept through a visit or just simply forgot, I always charged the full session fee for those missed appointments.

Some clients will become upset about this. Some might even stop seeing you because of it. But you deserve to protect your time, and you should be compensated appropriately for those missed appointments.

The First Three Sessions

It takes about three sessions for you and your client to start to really establish the beginning of the therapeutic relationship and for the client to get their whole backstory out on the table. In the very first session, I always focused on lots of compassionate listening, validation, and reassurance. The client has likely been waiting a long time to be seen, and they may have been holding these struggles and challenges inside for a lifetime. Clients often cry in the first session, and I would reassure and normalize that experience and say, "You're really feeling this and that's OK—this is a safe place for those emotions."

Clients also notice about halfway through the first visit that they might be jumping all over to give you many parts of their story. Sometimes they feel self-conscious about this. I also normalize this by saying something to the effect of, "In the first few sessions, we jump all over—it's OK—we're getting all of the pieces of the puzzle out on the table; keep going, I'm following."

After they share, I spend time reflecting back and validating, asking whether I got everything or whether I understood them correctly, then we dive in for more insight and to explore more details.

There's a delicate awareness of the passage of time in a session and the size and intensity of the container.

You want to be sure that if they are expressing something really important or they're processing through really deep emotion that you gently hold the edges of the session for them and make sure as you come to the last ten minutes that you're helping them feel prepared to transition out of your session and back into their lives beyond the clinical hour.

You wouldn't want to open up something super deep or push your client to explore something more intense knowing the session was about to end soon. And yet, you don't want to halt really good work or progress either. This is truly an art and a skill that you develop a muscle for over time. But consider where you are in the session timeline before you invite or ask a question of your client.

At the end of your session, you'll want to leave time to schedule the next session and sometimes we change that metric based on the level of acuity the client is experiencing. If they're in need of more support sooner, you can adjust your next appointment accordingly. If they're making a lot of progress, you can schedule them out every other week, for example.

What If I Don't Want to Work with a Client?

This is a controversial question that clinicians don't always agree on. I'll give you my take on this and how I've handled it over the years. I've been a therapist for twenty years, and there have been a couple of occasions where I did not feel I could be effective with a client I was working with, or they offended me or triggered me as a person. Sometimes it's very valuable to try to work out these issues of transference/countertransference with your own therapist or supervisor, and other times it's OK to refer the client out to another provider who might be a better fit.

Doing this can be really difficult for you and for the client. It's best if you can identify this issue within the first two to three visits before they get too far in the process. If it happens early on, you can simply say to the client that it's really important to you that they receive the best level of care for their needs, and after careful consideration, you've come to realize that you might not be the best provider for them. Or you could say that their needs are outside your area of expertise and provide them with three referrals to other providers who you think might be available and open to scheduling with them.

If it happens after you've worked together for a while, it can be more challenging to do this, but not impossible. I encourage therapists to try to work through their own issues around these types of clients first before referring out, but if in the end you feel that maintaining your therapeutic relationship would do more harm to the client than good or that the client is causing you hurt, suffering, high levels of irritation, or is disrespectful or unsafe with you, then you have every right to terminate the relationship and refer out.

When faced with this decision with a long-term client, I would try to express the need to transition care gently and with compassion, but also be honest and succinct. Remember that you're telling the client that you need to refer them out; you're not asking them for permission to do so.

There will be clients who challenge us, some whom we do not agree with, some who are difficult and draining to work with. There will also be clients whose stories cause us to feel secondary trauma or become triggered in our own stories. There are some clients who frustrate us and some who push our buttons.

That is par for the course in this industry.

That said, if you feel a sense of loathing just seeing their name on your schedule or you feel ongoing strong feelings of repulsion toward working with a client after you've spent some time and energy exploring your reaction with your own therapist or supervisor, then it is likely in the best interests of you and the client to terminate working together and refer them out.

These situations are very rare and may never happen to you as a therapist in private practice, but there's value in giving ourselves permission to realize that we have options if this does occur.

You are human and you may find on occasion that there's a client you just cannot work with for whatever reason, and if this happens, there are likely a lot of other providers who can step in and provide excellent care to that client.

CHAPTER 5

Define Your Niche, Establish Your Authority and Expertise

Defining Your Ideal Client

When building your private practice, it's important to have a well-defined area of specialty and expertise. In the very beginning, you're probably taking any client who reaches out to you for a session. But over time you start to develop your niche by refining who you like to work with and who you can be the most helpful to based on your area of expertise, training, interests, and educational background.

The more well defined your niche is, the easier it will be to identify your ideal client and market directly to them. Take some time to answer these questions to help you narrow down who your ideal client is:

- Who do you like working with the most?
- How would you describe this client? For example, age, family dynamics, socioeconomic status, educational background, and any other specific identifying factors you can think of.
- What problems does this ideal client face? How would they describe their current issues to you at the first visit?
- What do they need the most help with?
- What results are they looking for in therapy?
- What are their barriers to care?

- Do they have any objections that you can identify (reasons why they might not be able to start or continue therapy)?
- What treatment modality would be the most beneficial for this client (CBT, DBT, EMDR, etc.)?

Once you have answered these questions, you'll have a much better idea of how to describe your ideal client across all of your online "real estate" such as your website, Psychology Today profile, or other online directories as well as on rack cards and business social media pages.

It's OK to have a niche that covers more than one ideal client. Your niche might be two to four specialities. But the more refined and specific you are with understanding exactly who you want to work with, the easier it will be to attract those clients to your practice because they will see themselves in the description of your expertise and it will be much easier for them to convert to scheduling with you if that's clearly defined.

It's perfectly OK to identify who you really enjoy working with the most. Some therapists feel guilty or overly responsible for serving every client who reaches out to them for support. You do not have to be a generalist and specialize in serving everyone. In fact, that's not a great model for your business. Instead, it's best to consider who you feel really excited to work with. Who do you do your best work with? When do you feel like you're providing the most effective support?

On the flip side, it's also a good idea to identify the clients who you do not feel are a good fit for your expertise and training. There are a lot of needs across our industry. Our graduate degrees prepare us to serve a wide variety of client needs from ages one to one hundred with almost every diagnosable issue you can think of. But that does not mean that we should or have to serve every client who reaches out to us for help and support.

If this brings up uncomfortable feelings for you, I encourage you to consider that the clients who are not the best fit for you would be better served by someone who identifies those clients as *their* ideal client. Someone who has a special interest in working with those clients with those needs will be able to provide more effective support for those clients. It doesn't have to be you. The privilege of private practice is having the freedom to determine who you really want to focus on serving and developing a rewarding niche and specialty that feels like a great fit for both you and your ideal client.

Diving Deeper into Your Niche

Your niche might be best described as the age range of your client and their main concerns for seeking therapy. Are you working with young children who have anxiety issues? Is your niche middle-aged men with identity and depression issues? Do you specialize in working with couples, millennials, or older adults? Is your specialty supporting women with anxiety, for example?

Think for a moment about the ideal age range of your niche and what areas of care you want to really focus on as a provider.

This might change over time and that's OK too. And it may have a lot to do with your graduate education and internship or practicum experience. For right now, try to narrow down what age range and area of need might interest you the most.

Remember, when you narrow down the definition of your ideal client and identify your true niche and area of expertise, you're not limiting your scope of practice, but you're defining how you deliver your best work as a therapist, and that will help keep referrals coming your way and keep your caseload full.

Establishing Yourself as an Authority

Set Google Alerts for topics that are relevant to your area of expertise. For example, I set mine to women and depression, women and anxiety, mindfulness, self-care, and wellness. Google will send you a daily email with any new research, articles, and Google search results featuring your Google Alert words.

If you see relevant articles or news that is worthy of sharing, you can post those to your website and social media pages or share them in a newsletter with your clients and referral sources. When you do this on a regular basis, it's not only helping you stay up to date on the latest news or research in those areas but it's also helping your followers know that you are a trusted resource for the most up-to-date information on that specialty.

It's also a good idea to set a Google Alert for your name too. That way if anything is ever written about you online, you'll be the first to know about it.

When you blog or write articles or answer queries for quotes in articles, you're also expanding your depth as an authority too. One of the best ways to do this is through HARO queries. Visit HelpAReporter.com and sign up as a source. Three times a day, you will receive an email with a list of queries from reporters looking for quotes from sources on every topic under the sun.

Many are asking for quotes from mental health experts. I have successfully answered a lot of these queries over the years and have been featured in a lot of publications online and in print because of it. You simply click reply to the query you're answering and give the reporter your best quote. Most of the time the source will respond and let you know whether your quote was selected for their piece, but sometimes you will never hear back from them and the only way you'll discover you've been quoted is by the Google Alert you set up for your name.

You can also pitch to be a contributor for other well-known publications in our industry including Psychology Today, Thrive Global, Medium, HuffPost, and Psych Central.

Sometimes they will want a bio and headshot, which is why it's a good idea to have a press page on your website. On your press page, you should include a couple of different downloadable high-resolution professional headshots, a long- and short-form up-to-date bio, and any and all links to anywhere you've been quoted, seen, or heard in the media. This would include a link to every HARO query you were selected for, every podcast you've been a guest on, any TV or radio interview you were featured on, and any other professional media attention you've received.

If you are selected to be quoted in a HARO query, be sure to share that article when it goes live by tagging the journalist and the publication. Share this across all of your business social media platforms, LinkedIn page, and in your client newsletter if you have one. Then be sure to add that link to your press page. Over time, your press page will give a boost to your authority, especially as your list of media links grows.

Photos and Videos

Anytime you offer a presentation, find out whether there will be someone there capturing professional images or doing videography. At most large-scale conferences, there is usually a professional photographer who might be able to take pictures of you that you could use on your website.

Many times for my retreats and summits, I've hired professional photographers and videographers to capture the experience of my event. There is always a high return on this investment. The images can be used across all of your online spaces and instantly provide legitimacy and credibility to what you're offering and what you've built.

Many times when I was first doing public speaking gigs for free, I would ask for testimonials and photographs in exchange for my free presentation. The event or conference host was typically happy to provide these things to me, and over time I built a speaking page on my website that also increased my online authority. In addition, you can also ask the conference organizer or event host to connect you to two to three other contacts in their network who might be interested in having you present.

Media Kit

As your business expands beyond your 1:1 therapy work and you begin to scale, potentially building a platform and a coaching arm of your business, for example, you might find yourself in a position where you'll need a media kit.

Media kits are helpful when securing affiliate relationships with brands who are interested in partnering with you or sponsoring you or sponsoring your events or offers.

A media kit is essentially a one- to two-page full-color branded document that includes your professional headshot, a short bio of you with the highlights of your business achievements, and all of your stats on the size and demographics of your platform.

Sometimes brands are interested in working with you to get their product or service out in front of your audience or platform. You can leverage this desire by offering brand partnership or sponsorship opportunities with those companies. Sometimes you will get a percentage split of a sale made using your affiliate code for a product or service, and sometimes you will arrange a flat fee in exchange for advertising to your audience.

It goes without saying that when you get into the world of affiliates and brand partnerships, you would not be providing access to your therapy clients, but rather an audience you may have built on Facebook of people who are following you as an expert, but not working with you in a clinical setting or for psychotherapy services.

For example, I have formed a few affiliate and brand partnership relationships over the years with companies that are interested in getting their information in front of my Thriving Therapists audience. I have also had sponsors provide support at various levels of sponsorship for my large-scale summits and retreats in exchange for advertising opportunities that we provide to those sponsors.

These are only used for my coaching audience. Again, you would never establish brand partnerships for your clinical practice clients. It would be unethical to do so and could jeopardize your clinical license.

CHAPTER 6

Money and Entrepreneurial Mindset

In 1982, the Commodore 64 had just hit the market and it cost $595. The Commodore 64 was essentially a big computer keyboard and a joystick that you could connect to your TV to allow you to play video games. I was eight years old at that time, my parents were divorced, and I remember feeling like money was tight. But my sister and I were desperate to purchase this amazing device!

There was no way my parents could afford to purchase it, but that never stopped me from holding the vision that my sister and I would without a doubt own one someday soon. I never thought for one minute that we wouldn't get one. I only thought about what we could do to earn enough money to purchase it.

We became obsessed with the idea of buying it. We saved every single penny we received from any relative for our birthdays or holidays. We did every odd job we could to earn money toward this financial goal, but by far the most unbelievable effort we made toward this goal was creating something out of nothing to sell. We ended up painting the rocks in our driveway with little pretty designs on them and selling them to anyone who would buy from us. We literally went door to door selling painted rocks so we could purchase this cutting-edge video gaming device.

And we did it (with some assistance from our mom and grandma)! We actually bought one and hooked it up and played games on it and even learned how to build basic coding that would result in the computer system making a funny little sound on our TV.

This purchase provided us with hours and hours of joy! I still remember playing games on it with my sister and our neighborhood friends. Owning this device felt like we had cracked into a new dawn of computer technology. We were the cool kids. We had something super futuristic and technologically superior in our house. It felt so exciting to finally own one ourselves.

Why do I share this with you?

Because this story still lives in me today and it really brings up three distinct thoughts about my own money mindset that might be helpful to share:

1. I never think that I won't have enough money for something. I only think about how I will build or earn enough to make that purchase happen.
2. I believe I can earn money easily.
3. I always want to earn money doing things I really enjoy doing.

Number 3 brings up the reason why I love building other offers in my business such as retreats, culinary tours with my husband, courses, or coaching programs.

The opposite of this also feels true. For example, whenever I have done a job I do not enjoy doing, I feel like the money I earn just slips through my fingers. Like energetically it's much harder and more laborious to earn and somehow I never feel like it's enough. Like it's always too little, too late, or gone too soon.

What Is Your Money Mindset?

What does your negative money script sound like? "I can't afford that." "I worry I won't have enough." "What if this happens . . ."

Think about CBT. Your thoughts are *so* powerful. What you believe to be true about earning, saving, and spending money has a lot to do with how you feel about your finances and how you manage the money you have.

Let's consider this thought: what would it mean to you if you had a lot of money? If I said, "You will be a millionaire by this time next year," what comes up for you?

Do you have shame triggers around money? It's not uncommon for therapists to carry this extra sense of obligation or even a hero's complex to go out there and "save the world" and not require payment for it. That's simply not true and is totally unrealistic.

It can also be the fastest path to burnout for you as a therapist, and it definitely will not help you thrive.

When I think of thriving as a therapist, I think of living comfortably in abundance. I think about having a lot of time and money available to me. I think about having financial freedom and the freedom to do the things I really enjoy. To be able to afford those things in both dollars and hours.

Sometimes thoughts about increasing our earning potential can lead to feelings of shame or scarcity, and that can show up in a way that sounds like "I'm not worthy of earning that much money" or the flip side "Who do you think you are to consider yourself in that income bracket?"

You are worthy of working through these stories and triggers. Consider it a great investment in your financial future to dive into what might be holding you back when it comes to your money mindset as a therapist.

What Is Your Family Money Story?

Like many things in our adult perception, our financial story can be born out of how our families handled money and what their money mindset was too. Think back to what your family's money story was. How did your parents or caregivers talk about money? What was their narrative around spending and saving? Did you often hear a particular narrative around finances in your childhood home that may live inside you still today?

When I was growing up, my parents did not have a lot of money. We had to be wise about how we spent money and we certainly were not able to get whatever we wanted whenever we wanted it.

Interestingly enough, I never felt lacking. If I had dreams of attending a music summer camp or wanted to take private lessons for something, I remember that there was this feeling of "we cannot afford this, but we will find a way to make it happen." This belief translated into my core being and it still lives with me today. I never felt like I would have to miss out on going to camp or that we wouldn't be able to afford something, despite knowing that it was a stretch for my parents to make it happen.

This imprint of "we will find a way" has lived with me for decades. When I was broke, right out of grad school, raising two babies, and trying to build my practice, I never stopped dreaming that we would be able to buy Christmas gifts or take special family vacations. Even though many of our family trips were very inexpensive tent camping adventures and it was sometimes a struggle financially to make it happen, I lived with the knowledge that "we would find a way."

Why I Turned Down Four Million Dollars

In December of 2019, I was approached by a founder who had an idea to partner with me on a project to bring wellness programs that incorporated a robust mental health component to corporate America. His business proposal was appealing. He had a solid base of investors ready to support this concept, and he showed me in a series of business projections that after working together and scaling this company with him as his partner, we would expand this concept across the nation, sell it, and potentially earn between four and six million dollars in five years.

I sat with this pitch for many weeks. I called all of my trusted advisors and ran the numbers with them. Something in me felt like it was a no, despite the appeal of the potential earnings after the sale of this company. I just could not get my mind around partnering with him. I didn't think I would enjoy the work and I didn't think it would leave me with very much time to do the things I loved doing the most.

My friend is a financial planner and I took the pitch to her over lunch one day. She reviewed the projections really carefully with me and looked up and said, "Why can't you make this much on your own in five years?"

My head exploded!

It absolutely never occurred to me that it might be possible for me to be a multimillionaire on my own one day. But when she said it, I instantly felt invited to dream bigger for myself.

I ultimately declined the opportunity to partner with that founder, but what I gained out of that process was the shattering of my own glass ceiling.

What Else Do We Need in Order to Shift Our Money Mindset?

Anytime I start to fall down the scarcity rabbit hole, I swing back to abundance through my gratitude practices. Scarcity comes from feelings of lack or of not having enough. When I notice this in my thought pattern, I pause and try to reset into reviewing what I'm grateful for and all that I have and how far I've come.

This is not to dismiss that there are times when we need to make space for feeling fear or feeling scarcity. It can actually be productive for us to have a healthy review of what isn't working at the moment or areas we want to strengthen and improve.

But that said, I try to just allow myself to land there, not live there.

Remaining stuck in a scarcity mindset is not productive or inspiring for us. We cannot create new things or nurture new ideas from a space of lack or not enough. When we shift into practicing gratitude, we also shift into abundance. And when we're living from an abundant mindset, suddenly we feel this great sense of possibility and hope.

Another concept that helps our money mindset is having a clear vision of what we're creating and what we're hoping to build. I encourage you to find this space in places of stillness and quietude. I often meditate to clear my mind and create distance from my ego and doubt. In meditation, I can connect to a sense of truth and possibility. I can see what could happen for my business or my personal life. I get a clear vision of what I can create whether that is a retreat, a course, a summit, or a speaking opportunity.

Then I move from a visionary practice to implementation. I cast out a twelve-month business vision and develop a strategy to achieve my goals. I look at a year at a glance, usually on my giant wall calendar, and map out a plan for when I want to offer or launch something, then I work backward to see what needs to happen on a monthly, weekly, and daily basis in order to make that vision come to life.

The final thing that helps us with our money mindset is maintaining a focus on service rather than selling. When you keep yourself aligned with being in a place of serving your audience, it helps move you past any blocks that might be holding you back from putting your offer out into the world.

Sometimes therapists can feel indebted to service to a fault, and it can inhibit us from getting paid for our time, expertise, knowledge, and the products or services we develop for our clients. You deserve to be paid for your work. And at the same time, you need to remember that you're serving those who purchase from you because they want the information, experience, or educational knowledge that you're sharing with them.

Entrepreneurial Mindset

Entrepreneurs are distinguished by a few key characteristics. They have a keen awareness of identifying opportunities and they have a healthy amount of risk tolerance. They're quick learners, intrinsically motivated, and open to seeing things from another perspective. They tend to bounce back quickly from setbacks or mistakes. They see mistakes as learning opportunities to refine a process and make it better. They pay attention to the gaps in service and are eager to fill those.

The mindset of an entrepreneur is also one of limitless potential and creation. They do not set a ceiling on their earnings or creative potential. Strong entrepreneurial leadership can be infectious and contagious. They tend to operate from a positive, fun, and sometimes playful space, a willingness to try something and refine and repeat it if it works and toss it if it doesn't.

Entrepreneurs can easily burn out and become overwhelmed, so it's also critical that we take care of our self-care and boundaries (which will be discussed in detail in section 3 of this book).

In order to stay in a bright and edgy place of thinking of new, innovative ways of solving problems, it's also helpful to have practices and opportunities that inspire and push us to expand the way we perceive situations and how we approach them. I immerse myself in the arts by going to art museums and galleries, and I try new foods and love cooking new recipes. I dive into good books, new travel opportunities, live music, and social engagements with the most interesting people I can surround myself with on a regular basis. These experiences keep me feeling fluid and expansive rather than stuck in a rut or too routine.

Anytime I do these creative activities, I find that my daydreams, thoughts, and meditations are infused with new ideas and new ways to solve gaps or opportunities to create a program, product, service, or event for my audience.

Pay Attention

When we start to shift into an abundant money mindset and we harness our entrepreneurial energy, it can bring up unpleasant feelings for us. Can being a successful entrepreneur really coexist with being a therapist who deeply cares about providing service to clients in need?

Yes.

Pay attention to what comes up for you as your income increases as an entrepreneur. And remember that as you scale your income, you're increasing your reach and your impact too. You can also consider economies of scale where you can serve more people by providing a low-cost option (an inexpensive course, e-book, or webinar) where many people can access the information, but you as the creator still get paid well for your effort and knowledge.

Bottom line, it's OK to earn a great living as a therapist and you deserve to thrive in financial abundance.

INTRODUCTION TO SECTION 2
Scaling Your Business

I thought the definition of success as a psychotherapist was to fill every single slot on my caseload every single week. But I was wrong. This was actually the fastest path to burnout. I should know because I did this for ten years straight. I had thirty-five clients a week, seven clients a day with no break for lunch. I appreciated the income from this sizable caseload, but it came at a high cost to my well-being and work-life balance.

I remember feeling like I had nothing left to give to my husband or my kids by the end of a long week of client sessions. My head was so full from concentrating so intensely that I could not even make myself available to be present and connected with my precious family. In 2018/2019, I remember making a conscious decision to make a pivot to something different in my business. I decided not to allow myself to continue managing a caseload of this size anymore, but the transition to scaling my business didn't come easily either.

I only knew how to operate and identify as a therapist. My entire career identity was therapy. I did speaking gigs and retreats and workshops and some groups. I also led trainings and conferences, but the root of my core identity was being either a music therapist or a psychotherapist.

I couldn't fathom being a coach or course creator. I couldn't imagine running large conferences or summits for therapists or hosting a membership community. I didn't even know such things were possible for me. I didn't have any experience building a platform and couldn't even begin to imagine being in front of a camera. I was terrified of doing Facebook Lives and could not picture myself leading a movement of thriving therapists.

But it all started to shift for me when I drew a line in the sand and said, "No more!" I remember at the time proclaiming to my friends that "something has to change." I could literally feel my soul eroding inside of me. I had no time to pursue my creative passions, hobbies, or interests. I barely had time to make plans with friends. Taking time off and traveling felt impossible because where would I put all of these clients on my caseload? There were no open slots for months.

I remember following Stu McLaren on Facebook and deciding in April of 2019 to purchase his course on building a membership. I had started interacting in other Facebook groups for therapists, and I distinctly remember someone saying, "You seem to know a lot, you should start your own Facebook group!" So I did and in December of 2019, the Thriving Therapists Facebook community was born.

At that same time, I still had a full caseload and a long waitlist and then COVID-19 hit and I was buried under an avalanche of new referrals that I couldn't keep up with. At that moment, I decided it was time to build a group practice.

What I want you to know about this moment in time is that there is *no* good time to do anything in our businesses!

Busy business owners never suddenly have room to make big shifts; they just make the time and do it. I pivoted to telehealth like everyone else in the industry did at that time, I continued to nurture and get to know my Thriving Therapists Facebook community, and I hired my first therapist and built a group practice. As soon as her caseload was full, I hired the next therapist and rinsed and repeated that model over and over again as my group practice grew and grew.

I also stopped taking new clients and essentially bought back my time. We were able to serve more clients in need, but I didn't have to be responsible for serving those clients myself. And each time I finished working with a client, I never replaced them with a new client.

My caseload dropped significantly, but not at the expense of my income because I had created a group practice and a Facebook platform and started building additional streams of income for the Thriving Therapists Facebook community (such as courses, coaching programs, a membership community, in-person retreats, and summits).

Scaling has everything to do with increasing your impact and your income without burning out. My heart is in providing services for others. That's partly why I became a therapist. I was worried that I wouldn't be able to stay in the field because seeing so many clients every week was too much for me, but I also didn't want to sacrifice the income.

Now I've learned how to serve thousands of therapists who are turning around to build thriving practices in their own communities, thereby increasing access to outpatient mental health care to clients in need, and together we're creating a ripple effect of change.

How Does This Apply to You?

If you've landed on section 2 of this book, you're already thinking about moving beyond the 1:1 model of care as a therapist and there are so many ways you can do this! In this section, we will cover how to build group therapy programs so you can serve more clients in less time. We will also cover retreat building, how to build an online course, how to build a group practice, how to pivot to coaching, and how to build a speaking arm of your business. We will also cover how to outsource and hire a team, how to build a platform, and how to secure brand partnerships or affiliate sponsors too.

Remember that scaling your business as a coach likely means you'll create a second company that separates these offers from your clinical license. You'll learn to include disclaimers and have the right liability waivers in place for your offers and that not all clients are appropriate for scalable offers. When you start to scale as a therapist, it's important to be sure that you either build a completely new coaching or wellness business, for example, or know the bounds of your clinical license.

Most of what we're covering in this section of the book is designed to help you pivot away from the clinical 1:1 model of psychotherapy work and expand into coaching and wellness offerings for your customers or clients who seek these services. It's really critical that you understand as you make this shift into building scalable offers that you're moving away from the confines of your role as a clinician and moving into the role of a coach, educator, facilitator, content creator, or retreat leader, for example.

While I use the term clients interchangeably here with students, customers, or consumers, please note that the scaleable aspects of your work are distinctly separate from your work as a psychotherapist bound by your code of ethics and licensure requirements.

There's a lot to learn about scaling, so let's dive in!

CHAPTER 7

Building Groups

Early on in my solo practice, I heard an echo from my clients. They were lonely and craved connection and community. Many of them were discussing how they longed for opportunities to be with other like-minded women doing interesting things, but they didn't know where to find these types of opportunities.

When we do anything related to scaling our business, it's really important that we listen to the audience in front of us. What are they asking for? What do they want? What do they need?

We can sit in our offices all day long and craft up the most amazing offers from group therapy programs to online courses to retreats to trainings, but it could be very hard to sell them to anyone unless you have actually heard from people that they want this or need this from you.

I knew that I had about ten to twelve clients on my caseload all describing the same desire. They wanted to be part of interesting, creative, and meaningful circles. That's when I decided to build a series of women's community events. This was my first attempt at creating something outside of my 1:1 clinical work. I didn't understand the coaching and wellness business world, but I knew that these had to be offers that were completely separated from my therapy business and I knew I had to structure them as cash fee wellness offers. I also knew I had to have liability waivers signed by each client stating that they understood these events were not psychotherapeutic in nature and were not meant to replace any medical treatment. I also had them sign consent forms, and I put disclaimers all over my marketing materials to really distinguish this from my clinical work and protect my license.

I organized several different events over a series of a few months. We had a pottery class one evening, a cooking class, a tai chi class, a tea tasting at a tea shop, and a meditation class. The attendees absolutely loved trying these different classes, and for some, it sparked a new hobby or interest. For others, it addressed their need to connect with others and learn something new.

Later in my career, I started to build group programs. These were designed the same way. Not clinical. Not run through insurance. Not meeting medical necessity or addressing symptom management. I used the same liability waivers, disclaimers, and consent forms, and these group programs were also designed as cash fee offers, meaning not run through their medical insurance. These were designed as wellness groups, and I built them as a two-hour offering for about ten women in each session.

The idea was that if I offered a group session on Wednesday evenings, for example, then I would be able to open up some of my 1:1 slots on Wednesday morning and not replace them with new clients. The group would supplement that income loss, and I would essentially make what I would make in four individual sessions in one evening group with ten women.

This is how we buy back time.

Take a moment now and think about your existing caseload. What are four to five topics that you find yourself discussing, processing, or reviewing with the majority of your caseload on a regular basis? Do you often work on communication issues, self-care, boundary management, emotional regulation or distress tolerance skill building, self-esteem or self-awareness? These could all be turned into a skill building group or group wellness program.

What are the biggest concerns your clients have now? Maybe you specialize in grief and loss, depression, or anxiety? Almost anything you work on in an individual session can be translated into a group session.

Maybe you want to get creative and add other elements to your group offerings? Perhaps you want to include yoga, art making, guided imagery, or meditation? Maybe your group program will culminate in a weekend retreat? Or your weekend retreat ends and people want continuity and you build an ongoing group for them after the retreat.

Think about what comes before and after your scaling offers too. You know when you read a great book and then it ends and you immediately try to find out what other books that author has written so you can read another one from the same author? That's oftentimes how your clients feel about your scalable offers. When one offer ends, it's nice to consider what else you can offer them if they want more from you.

Building Your Group

There are lots of things to consider when building group programs.

- What is the theme of your group?
- Who needs this group and what problems do they have?
- How long will your group be? One, two or three hours long?
- How many weeks will you offer your group for?
- What will your group cost and how will they pay for it (one week at a time or all at once?)?
- How many participants do you want in your group?
- What is your cancellation policy?
- How will you handle it if a group member is no longer appropriate for the group?
- Will your group be a closed or open group?
- Will you have a curriculum or teaching materials?
- What will attendees need to bring to group?
- Will this be held virtually or in person?
- Do you have the correct forms in place for your group (waivers, disclaimers, and consents)?

When I built my women's groups, they were only supposed to be held for six weeks, and each time we got to the end of another six-week session, sometimes one or two members would decide to drop out and one or two new people would want to join our group.

The six-week session that I built went on consecutively with very few breaks for over two years. I enjoyed facilitating the group as much as the women enjoyed attending. I offered it to ten women and charged $40/session. We opened with a check-in and went around the room to see how their week was going. I would give them journal prompts for them to reflect on and write answers to in their journals. Then we would set our intentions and do a twenty-minute shamanic journey or meditation exercise. After the meditation, they would journal their insights. Then when everyone was ready, we would go around the circle again and share a summary of their experience and what powerful learning or knowing they'd gained from their meditation. We would end with an intention or affirmation for the week ahead and close our circle.

I always had hot tea and water for them. I lit a candle, put the chairs in a circle, and had meditation cushions and yoga blankets too. I had relaxing music playing when they arrived and would sometimes even burn lavender incense in the room before we started. The group felt like a supportive, safe space where women could come, be fully seen and heard, go inward for insight and awareness, return to their sense of truth and knowing, and go back out into the world feeling mentally and emotionally stronger and more capable.

Structuring Your Group

There are pros and cons to how you structure your groups. My groups were always structured as closed groups. I did not want new people coming into our group once we made it past the first couple of sessions. Similar to therapy, I found that people would build a trusting relationship with me and with the other members of the group, and after the original stories have been shared and bonds begin to form, it's difficult to fold new members in and go back to allow members to get to know each other all over again.

Some groups are structured more like ongoing educational sessions and do not require group members to do a lot of interpersonal sharing.

These types of groups could be run as open groups and allow new members to join at any time. But it's important to consider what type of group you're developing and that will help inform you on how best to structure your group design.

How Long Should One Session Be?

This all depends on how many attendees you have and what you're doing in your group. Are you asking ten people to share their thoughts or insights? If so, it takes time to get around a circle without rushing. I would suggest for groups of ten members that your group be between ninety minutes and two hours long to allow time for sharing. If you are teaching something to your group or focusing on skill building, then the sessions can be shorter in length than a process- or sharing-based group.

Are you doing an activity like a yoga session or making art? I always allow more time for activity-based sessions because people want to talk before and after the actual activity and again, you do not want people to feel rushed.

One of the most common mistakes in group design (and retreat or workshop building too) is overscheduling. We often think that we need more in our agenda when in actuality less is almost always more when it comes to facilitating group sessions. People crave space, and because much of our lives are so overscheduled, it feels nurturing and restorative to allow presence and connection to be the focus of your gathering rather than a tightly run agenda or program.

This is not to say that you don't have a plan. You need to have a clear vision for how your group will be structured and how each session connects to the one before it and the one after it.

Understanding your theme is also important. Ultimately, you need to be able to answer these questions:

- What problem is this group addressing?
- What results are my group members hoping for?
- How does this group help support those results or help solve the problem my attendees have?

- Do all attendees feel safe, welcome, and like the group is beneficial for them?
- Is there anything you can do as the group facilitator to make this a better experience for your attendees?

How to Facilitate Your First Session

Even though this isn't a therapy group, your therapeutic knowledge will serve you well when facilitating your groups. When I open a new group, I make a point to warmly welcome each attendee as they arrive and make them feel comfortable. If I am hosting in a brick-and-mortar office space, I tell them where they can put their things, encourage them to help themselves to tea or water, and advise them where the restrooms are located.

If I'm hosting a group virtually, I welcome them, ask them to drop their name and something about themselves in the chat, remind them how to prepare their space to get the best experience from their virtual group, and remind them to keep their camera on and mute themselves unless we're sharing.

Before I start a new group, I also set an intention that the group attendees will benefit from this offering and that I will remain grounded and aware of the needs of the group as I guide and lead the group.

When I open a group, I always begin by addressing confidentiality. I let members know that what happens inside our group should remain private and confidential. I encourage them to bring their whole selves to the group experience, that they can leave their inhibition and judgment at the door, that this is a place for deep restoration, insight, awareness, learning, and growth—or whatever the group is meant to provide. I help them understand some simple group rules around making sure all members feel heard and seen, that we try to avoid cross-talking or monopolizing, etc. I explain my role and my experience and background too so they can trust that I am facilitating this group and they're entering a safe container.

I always encourage everyone to take care of their own needs during the group and remind them that even though this isn't designed as a therapy group, sometimes emotions come up and that all of our feelings and experiences are welcome in the group. I invite them to remove distractions, turn their phones off if they can, and protect the time they've established for this group process. And finally, I end the opening with the reminder that if at any time someone finds they need more support, I can help guide them to those referrals and resources.

Opening the Circle

After I review all of the orientation rules above, we go around the circle to introduce ourselves, sharing what we would like to get out of this group experience and what made them sign up for this group.

After that, you can ask participants to share answers to some questions you have for them or give them a journal prompt to write their answers to. When ten people share, it can take over thirty minutes to move through one question, so plan accordingly. Journal prompts work well for larger groups because they can write a long answer silently and share a short synopsis with the group when you go around the circle.

Middle of the Group

The middle of the group is the meat of your sandwich. This is where you can do the bulk of your teaching, processing, or the activity you're offering. Leave plenty of time for this portion of your group. If your group is a two-hour group, you could have thirty minutes for the opening portion, one hour for the middle section, and thirty minutes left for the closing.

Closing the Group

I typically end my group by going around and having each person set an intention for the week or having participants share one goal they would like to hold between now and the next session. You can have them reframe something they said or felt about themselves that they may have shared at the beginning of the group. And always remind members of the time and date of the next session at the end of each group.

Disclaimers and Cancellation or Refund Policies

Be sure to include a disclaimer on your marketing materials that this is a "wellness group and not meant to be a replacement for psychotherapy or medical treatment." You also need to create a liability waiver form and have participants sign when they register for your group. Be sure to also include your cancellation and/or refund policy. I recommend saying "Due to the extensive nature of planning involved in this group therapy program, refunds cannot be provided." Or determine when you will provide a refund such as a 50 percent refund up to X date, or no refunds after X date, for example.

It takes a lot of time to plan a group and keep your group details organized. If you have people signing up and canceling, this requires work and extra marketing on your end to fill those lost spaces. You should be paid accordingly for that time and labor. Be sure to also outline your policy for missing sessions due to illness and how participants can reach you between sessions if they need to let you know they cannot attend.

Building a Separate Company for Your Scaleable Offerings

I do recommend building a separate coaching/wellness business to keep all of your scaling offers separate from your clinical practice. We will go into more detail about this later, but essentially you will need the following:

- LLC or PLLC (if your state allows you to form one or register this company as the appropriate business structure—check with your accountant and attorney to get their trusted council on this)
- EIN
- Website domain name (I usually secure this through GoDaddy)
- Business bank account (I recommend one checking and two savings for any business you have as discussed in chapter 1)
- Square and/or Stripe business account
- Business PayPal account
- Business email
- QuickBooks or bookkeeping system

When I first started running groups many, many years ago, I did not have a separate business for these offerings, but eventually I created my second company for these types of offerings. If I had to do it all over again now, I would absolutely create a second company from the very beginning for the sake of organization and protection.

Marketing Your Group

Marketing can be where some therapists start to feel overwhelmed. We're fine when it comes to building the group and facilitating a group session, but when it comes to marketing and launching our group, that's where sometimes we start to feel lost. Don't worry though, this process can be simple.

When I started my first group offerings, all I did was send out a blind carbon copy email that included info about the group I was offering and asked people to email me back if they were interested in registering. Once I heard back from enough participants, I either sent them a business PayPal invoice or built a business invoice in my Square account.

Once I started doing more of these types of things, I learned how to build landing pages and sales pages on my website. Creating a sales page is a great way to share your offer with more people and create more legitimacy for your group or offer that you're building. You can add images, descriptions, payment buttons, and back-end automations or workflows that will make your process more streamlined and save time and energy for you, the facilitator. The more you can systemize or automate, the easier it will be for you to rinse and repeat these offers over and over again in the future.

If you feel overwhelmed by the tech side of things, these are tasks that can be outsourced. Spend your time creating the concept and the content and designing the program and offer and find support for the other aspects of your launch. You can hire virtual assistants or other experts to assist you with everything from designing the marketing materials to building websites or landing pages for you.

At first, if you want to keep it super simple, you can start with an email and an invoice for payment.

As far as the timeline for building and launching your group goes, I would estimate that you need three to four months to successfully design, build, and fill your group program. Sometimes people need to see your offer five to seven times before they make a decision. And they need plenty of time to schedule your group session into their busy lives. Sometimes people also need to save up for the cost of your offer, so you wouldn't want to build something and then expect to run it immediately or just within a month. Give yourself plenty of time to design something amazing. It will feel good not to be rushed or pressured to fill your group.

Where Can You Share Your Offer?

Share it everywhere! The more you share your offer, the faster you will fill it.

- Share it inside your email newsletter.
- Share it all over your social media pages (both business and personal accounts).
- Share it with other therapists, providers, or coaches in your network.
- Share it on your LinkedIn page.
- Add your group info to your automatic email signature.
- Create a rack card and share with your referral sources.
- Invite a therapist to co-facilitate something with you and then you can cross-promote it and fill it together.

Creating a Back-End Offer Once Your Group Is Finished

As I mentioned, sometimes one five- or six-week session might continue into the next five- or six-week session and so on. But if your group feels complete and you find that the last session feels like a natural place to stop or close your group, then consider what else you can offer your participants. These group attendees have likely established a lot of trust in you during their time in your group and they may want to continue receiving support from you beyond the group.

You could create a back-end offer such as

- A one-day workshop
- A weekend retreat
- A mastermind program (more intensive, smaller group, usually higher priced)
- An e-book or printed book
- An online course
- 1:1 coaching
- A "level 2" group that takes people to the next level from wherever they finished off with your first group

Ultimately, groups create a sense of community support that clients cannot get in 1:1 work with you. What they gain from other members is invaluable! They see themselves across the circle in what others are sharing and learning. They feel even more seen and heard than they would in 1:1 therapy or coaching work. As the facilitator, you're increasing your impact and your income by scaling to a group instead of only doing 1:1 session work.

Groups are a great way to start building additional streams of income, and you can build them and offer them in person or online. I hope you'll try building your own!

CHAPTER 8

Hosting Retreats

This chapter easily could be an entire book! I've spent the past two decades leading retreats locally, nationally, and internationally and have a lot of great information to share with you to help you design, build, and launch your transformational, sold-out retreat.

In this chapter, we will be covering eight sections on retreat building including casting the vision, budgeting time and money, selecting a venue, designing your retreat offer and creating the perfect agenda, marketing for success, considering your liability and the required information you need from guests, protecting yourself as the facilitator, and finally learning how to trust the process.

Get ready to learn everything you need to know about designing the retreat of your dreams!

Let's get started . . .

Casting the Vision

Many therapists and coaches start retreat planning with a location in mind first. They start getting attached to the beauty of where they want to host something before they even create the vision for what they're building. I think it's best to start from the very beginning and consider your broad vision and mission before thinking about where you want to host your first retreat.

First, consider who you're building this retreat for and what the theme of your retreat will be. If you get very clear on this, the marketing and other retreat building elements will be much easier for you. It's a good idea to consider the audience that is right in front of you. What are they asking you for? Why would they want to sign up for a retreat? What do they need the most out of a retreat experience? There are many options here.

You can build a retreat that is almost exclusively designed for rest and restoration, or one that is full of adventure and activities. You can build a retreat that is designed around self-care and wellness themes, for example, or one that is teaching guests a new skill like various types of yoga or meditation techniques. You can even build a retreat that is part education and part restoration, which is what I've done for my Thriving Therapists audience.

The ideas and options are truly endless. But when you begin by considering who you're building your retreat for, this will guide you in selecting your venue and location. If, for example, your audience is interested in deep rest and restoration, you would want to search for a venue that's far removed from the stimulation and noise of a busy town or city and a venue that has luxurious rooms and bedding. If your audience is full of thrill seekers looking for lots of activities and adventure opportunities, then this will guide you to a location offering loads of amenities and excursions for your guests.

For many years when I was working as a full-time psychotherapist in private practice, I hosted retreats for my clients. It all started when I heard many of my busy working mom clients say, "What I wouldn't give for a day to myself!" Many of my clients were calling out for a self-care and wellness day, which led me to the idea of creating one-day workshops for my clients. From there, they asked for weekend retreats, and from there, I built my first international retreat with a colleague back in 2012.

Listen to the audience in front of you.

What are they asking for? Build your offers and retreats and programs to fill the gap that they've identified needing. You're more likely to sell something to a group of people who are calling out for a program, service, or product from you than if you dream up something from scratch assuming that people will sign up for it.

Once you've identified who you're building it for and what the theme will be, then it's much easier to identify ideal venues and locations. When planning your first weekend or weeklong retreat, remember that it takes time to do this. I recommend for a weekend retreat giving yourself at least five months of planning time, and for a weeklong retreat, sometimes you need ten months to a year depending on where you're hosting and the demand for excellent venues. Some of the international venues I book now require more than a year out for reservations.

Budgeting Time and Money

When budgeting for a retreat, you must spend some time calculating your time and financial investments before you build anything for your audience. Planning a really successful, sold-out retreat takes time. It isn't just the weekend or week you're hosting. It can be five to ten months or a year of work depending on the size and scale of your offer or the size of your platform you're marketing this to. For more on platform building, see chapter 14.

First, ask yourself how much you want to make for your time and expertise during the actual retreat itself. Then double that amount to consider the time it takes to design, build, and launch your retreat leading up to the hosting time.

Once you have that number, then start to consider all the costs you will incur for hosting this retreat. It's critical that you calculate the costs before you set your pricing for guests.

Typical Costs for Hosting a Retreat

- Your venue (does this include meals or will food and beverages be an extra expense?)
- All the extras for your venue (such as any upcharges for service fees, tax, gratuities, use of utilities, heating of the pool or hot tub, air-conditioning fees, cleaning fees, international tourism tax, deposit

requirements, even extra charges for water use or per person charges over a certain number of guests)
- Any additional team members (such as yoga instructors, chefs, assistants, massage therapists, guest speakers, photographers, etc.)
- Gifts for guests (as simple as a small branded notebook and pen or as extravagant as a group excursion or spa service)
- Transportation costs (getting to and from the retreat location, your airfare, staff airfare, ground transportation for you and your team and for guests, rental car or shuttle buses/vans)

My magic formula when calculating retreat pricing is to add up all of my costs and add a five to ten percent buffer for the costs you may have that you're not even aware of, then divide by the number of attendees and double that amount as the price per guest. This gives you enough of a cushion for extra fees and unexpected expenses and leaves you with enough room to still make a profit too.

Selecting a Venue

Venue selection plays a very significant role in retreat planning, marketing, and budgeting. You should expect to spend a lot of time on finding the very best venue for your guests and for your price point. You should also expect to dig deep into your research to read all of the reviews you can find of your property and find as many photos and videos of your venue as you can if you cannot visit before you decide to book it to host there.

For the purpose of this chapter, we will be covering weekend and weeklong retreat venue selection. One-day retreats do not include many of these considerations. That said, selecting a venue for your one-day retreat or workshop is just as important as overnight retreats too.

For weekend or weeklong retreats, you have two major options. You can select to rent an exclusive private property or retreat center that is only going to be used at that time by your group of guests, or you can select a hotel or resort where your guests would be sharing space with other guests of the property. There are pros and cons to each of these choices. It all depends on what your vision is and how you want to design your retreat.

I have hosted retreats at both exclusive properties and at resorts. I honestly like both of them for very different reasons. Exclusive properties provide you with a sense of privacy and a really confidential, safe space for deep process work and transformation. Guests really relax into the luxury of knowing that the only other people they will encounter at the pool or at mealtimes are other retreat participants. Knowing this affords you and your guests this very special, safe container that you cannot replicate at a hotel or resort where there are other non retreat guests around at all times.

However, sometimes hosting at a resort can be easier for you as the facilitator because the lodging, cleaning, meals, and some resort amenities are all taken care of for you and your guests. You don't need to worry about Airbnb rules for closing up the property at the end of use or bringing in your own chef, and many resorts offer a wide variety of amenities that you cannot afford to add on to a private rental property such as guided hiking into beautiful locations, full-service spa amenities, concierge services, or even classes on the property such as yoga, tai chi, sound bath healings, drum circles, or excursions they can help you organize for adventure or to see local attractions.

Hosting in a resort or hotel usually means you would rent a conference room for your programming and retreat sessions that you're hosting. Consider those costs when calculating your budget. Sometimes resorts will offer you a flat room rental fee and other times they calculate this based on the food and beverage spend for your group. You can submit an RFP (request for proposal) from the resort or hotel venue and let them know the anticipated size of your group, how many rooms you would need to book, how many nights you plan to be there, what type of property amenities you anticipate using, and your overall budget for this retreat. They should send you back a proposal, which you will want to review carefully. Read the fine print. You don't want to be caught off guard with charges you weren't expecting. You also want to be sure you're clear whether the guest hotel rooms are being charged to the guests or to your master account.

Whether you're getting ready to sign a contract with a retreat venue or a resort, remember that everything can and should be negotiated. You should ask about discounts or ask that certain charges be waived or other amenities be included for your guests. I have negotiated many contracts with exclusive retreat centers and with large-scale resorts. Most are willing to work with you, and you only have one shot to get the very best deal possible for you and your guests.

What to Consider When Selecting a Venue

- Does the property offer private and/or shared rooms?
- Does the property offer private and/or shared bathrooms?
- Does the property have comfortable space for facilitating group sessions?
- How far are you from the nearest airport and hospital?
- How safe is your location of choice?
- Where will you stay as the facilitator?
- Can you see photos of every single bedroom they offer (for private Airbnb or exclusive property rentals)?
- What is the setup for the kitchen and dining room?
- How close are you to the property next to you? What is close by?
- How does the property handle deposits, payments, and final balances? Wire transfer or credit card payment options?
- What is their cancellation policy?

All of these considerations have come to my attention from personal experience hosting retreats. Some guests want the option to have a private room, but if you only have a venue with a limited number of bedrooms, it might not be possible to offer a private room without a significant single supplement upcharge.

Sometimes, things do not always go as planned. When I hosted my second retreat in Costa Rica, I became extremely ill. Luckily, my colleague was able to host the group sessions in my absence because I was completely incapacitated for many days. I was bedridden, incredibly weak, very sick, and unable to eat any food for many days on end. I ended up losing seventeen pounds in seven days.

The venue owner wanted me to go to the hospital, but I refused knowing how far it was to get there. Instead, they sent a private ambulance to come to the property to attend to my medical needs. They administered IV fluids to me in my bedroom. This service could only be paid for in cash in US dollars. Luckily I'm always prepared and had brought several hundred dollars with me. In a nutshell, knowing where the closest hospital is is on the list above because of this very challenging personal experience. In addition, it's also a very good idea when hosting internationally that you consider cohosting with a colleague or bringing an assistant with you in the event of these types of emergencies.

Also having a room for yourself that is far enough away from the attendees is critical. When hosting retreats, you can feel like you're "on" 24/7. It's really important to allow yourself space and time away from the group to recharge. If your room is directly next door to guests' rooms, you might feel like you never fully have the privacy and break that you need to rest and replenish as the leader of your group.

Making sure that the Airbnb host or exclusive retreat center property owner sends you photos and/or videos of each room of the venue is really critical. I once hosted a culinary tour with my husband for our company, Gunnell Innovation, at a gorgeous villa in Tuscany. There were twelve rooms in the villa, but the property listing only showed eleven bedroom photos. When I asked them to send me photos of that twelfth bedroom, I could see that it was on the very top floor in a room with slanted ceilings because it was literally under the roofline of the villa. This was really important for me to be able to see beforehand because not every guest would be comfortable in a room with slanted ceilings or a room that required three flights of stairs to get to.

The more you research and find out before you book, the more prepared you are to answer questions from your guests and to market your retreat in a super honest and authentic way.

I've seen retreats hosted by facilitators that show the most shocking bedroom arrangements. Some look like youth hostels, where ten guests would share a room. There's nothing wrong with a "bunk room" setup, but you certainly cannot be charging your guests top dollar for "luxury accommodations" when you're selling something super basic like wooden bunk beds for multiple guests to share.

Bottom line, you're building trust in your brand with everything you do from your social media posts to your emails to your products, programs, services, and offers. The more you know about the retreat venue that you're selling, the more you can stand behind the price point and the more your guests will trust your brand and develop brand loyalty with you over time.

Designing Your Retreat Offer and Creating the Perfect Agenda

Once you've identified who you're building this retreat for, what the theme is, and what the timeline, budget, and venue will be, then it's a good idea to spend some time considering what your retreat will offer to your guests. If you've identified the problem area of your ideal guest, then begin to design the retreat to be part of a solution to that problem.

Answer the call of your prospective guests. Consider why they might sign up to attend your retreat. What do they need the most right now and how will your retreat provide that for them? Then it's critical that you get very clear on what your retreat guests will learn or experience during the retreat and what they can expect to feel or know by the end of the retreat.

This will guide you in developing the perfect agenda for your retreat.

A common mistake I see when I offer coaching to those who want to learn how to successfully build retreats is they overschedule and pack their agenda with tons of plans. Most people attend retreats to relax and restore and get away from feeling overwhelmed and overscheduled. They want to quite literally "retreat" and get away from their busy, everyday lives. Leave lots of downtime for guests to seek stillness, integrate, process, rest, and restore, but also be sure to strike the right balance of engagement and offer things to do too.

I remember planning my first international retreat. I think I brought enough material to teach a graduate-level course on self-care and wellness! But we only had one week with our guests, and I was co-facilitating with my colleague, which meant we each only had a couple of group sessions with our guests in total. The rest was simply inviting them to slow down, enjoy morning yoga sessions, get a spa treatment or massage, lay around and soak in the stunning infinity pool overlooking the ocean, walk the grounds and awaken their senses, enjoy delicious meals, meditate, rest, nap, play, and make connections with other guests.

A strong retreat facilitator also pays careful attention to the energy and dynamic of the group as a whole. Be prepared to shift gears if your group energy dictates something different from what was on your original agenda. There are many times I made a game day decision on swapping out an evening candlelight yoga session for a high-energy drum circle if the energy of the group warranted a pivot.

You should have enough ideas in your back pocket for your group that you're prepared to offer various sessions during your retreat, but you should also be tuned-in enough to your group to determine when you need to mix up the order of offerings to be aligned with what the group seems to need most from you in that moment.

There were times it was so hot in Costa Rica that we decided to lead a process group in the pool! And other times we extended a group session or pushed back a meal time when the group wanted to go longer with mask making or mandala work, for example.

All retreats seem to have a natural arc to them. There's a starting point, a rise in energy to a peak, and then a descent down to a beautiful resolution. As you host more and more retreats, you'll recognize these patterns too and you'll be able to accommodate your group and their needs with ease and expertise.

I always open every retreat with a really fun physical icebreaker that gets people up on their feet, moving and laughing. This seems to break down any nervous energy guests feel upon arrival. Then I go over a complete retreat orientation including house rules, boundaries, and expectations, and I invite guests to give themselves permission to get as much as they can out of their retreat experience.

If you build a safe container and metaphorically "set the table" for your guests, transformative growth and change can happen.

As therapists, we're trained to facilitate groups, and it's always good to review group dynamics with your guests such as the importance of allowing equal time for guests to share and process, that you value reflective listening and validation, that no one has to "rescue" anyone else, and that you aim to limit cross-talking or monopolizing. I usually explain that there's a ton of power in just witnessing what someone is sharing and that it's not necessary to fix, solve, or share after someone speaks their truth. It's also important that you remind your guests that this retreat is not designed to replace therapy or medical treatment.

When it comes to setting your agenda, you'll want to leave lots of room for transitions, meal times, and lots of breaks to allow your guests to choose what feels right to them at that moment. This level of freedom over our downtime is such a gift in a busy person's life. When do we ever get to just decide spontaneously how we want to use a free two-hour window? It's a rarity that there are unfilled hours in our lives.

I would only offer a maximum of two structured groups a day while on retreat and only for a maximum of three hours each. Anything more than that, you risk draining your guests and making the retreat feel more like work than it is replenishment.

I believe firmly that all transformational retreats should include elements of the sacred and profound. How will you build in ritual, ceremony, or opportunities for creative connection? Will you have an opening or closing ceremony? Will you acknowledge the land and the people who have been in this space before you? Will you include any reference to the environment around you? The ocean, mountain, jungle, or even the moon cycles? I have intentionally hosted retreats around a full moon and have offered sacred fire burning ceremonies, drum circles, and profound meditation sessions.

The mystical and magical energy of retreat work should not be missed by you or your guests.

Marketing for Success

Ideally, you will be able to market your retreat to your own platform or audience you've developed and it will be so beautifully designed and priced so perfectly that it will sell out very quickly.

Remember that photos and stories sell. If you've never hosted a retreat before, ask the venue to send you any high-resolution images you can share to give your audience an idea of what it will look and feel like to stay at this beautiful property. Always invest in bringing a photographer with you or hiring a local photographer near your retreat venue to capture the spirit and beauty of what you're creating.

We brought a professional photographer with us for our very first retreat in Costa Rica and used those images to sell all of our subsequent retreats much faster and easier because people could really picture what it would be like to be a guest on a retreat in Costa Rica.

Building safety for your guests begins with your marketing plan.

Be clear about what your retreat is offering, what it's designed for and what it is not designed for, what the purpose is, what results your guests can expect, what your rules or boundaries are around alcohol use, what they can expect regarding exclusive private space usage vs. a resort with other guests, and include a disclaimer that your retreat is not a substitute for medical treatment or therapy. You should also be very clear in all of your marketing materials what your cancellation policy is and have guests agree to those terms or sign a form that acknowledges that they understand your policy when paying their deposit or paying in full for their retreat.

Each retreat you host helps you build the next one. You want to be sure to get testimonials from guests, and the time to ask them for one is not when they get home. Be sure to ask guests to complete a testimonial for you somewhere between the middle and the end of your retreat when you are three-quarters of the way through with your offering. That's when people will take the time to share an amazing review while they are still immersed in all of the beauty, awe, and wonder of your retreat and while what they're sharing is still really fresh in their lived experience of your retreat.

A good strategy for launching your retreat is to create some excitement before you open registration. Email your prospective guests or post some photos and stories on your social media pages with a countdown to when your registration is open. I have done this strategy several times and even had a weekend retreat for ten guests sell out within five minutes of the open cart.

Nothing feels better than selling out your retreat and having a waitlist in case someone cancels or a waitlist for the next one. If you develop a smart marketing strategy and share your excitement and enthusiasm for what you've built, people will feel energized to join you.

Considering Your Liability and the Required Information You Need from Guests

It's critical that you protect yourself and your guests when hosting retreats, and one way to be sure to do this is by having a lawyer draft a liability waiver for your guests to sign upon registering for your retreat offering.

Your liability waiver should include detailed sections around risk, health and safety, injury, or even death. It should mention that your offer is not considered a substitute for medical treatment and is not psychotherapeutic in nature, and it should release you from all liability related to your clinical work as a therapist. You can add sections about your cancellation policy and use of words or images for future marketing purposes, as well as sections on personal property and medical care consent if a guest is injured on retreat. Your lawyer will draft this up in accordance with your local laws, and while it is a significant investment to create this initial document, it's not something you can afford to skip.

This is also a business expense and can even be rolled into your budget considerations when calculating what the cost will be per person for your first retreat. For subsequent retreats, you should be able to edit and have your attorney review and use the same document again without a large amount of time, energy, or financial investment.

Required Information You Need from Your Guests

- Signed copy of your liability waiver
- Photo release
- Emergency contact info

- Copies of passports if hosting internationally
- Allergies you should know about (food, medical, or environmental)
- Medical or health issues, injuries, or limitations you should know about
- A medication reminder to guests to bring all prescription meds in the prescription bottles for proof if required at security as well as any over the counter medications they think they may need while on retreat
- Anything that is required by the venue (some international venues require date of birth, full name, and copy of passport for all guests)

Things You Can Provide for Your Guests

- A detailed packing list of what to bring and what to leave behind
- Items that the venue has for them (toiletries, beach towels, hair dryers)
- Instructions on how to prepare for their retreat
- Reminders about the accommodations (for example, no air-conditioning but fans in rooms, that there are many steps to get to the bungalows, that the villa is located next to a church and they will hear church bells on the hour)
- Invitations for aftercare or integration opportunities after the retreat

Protecting Yourself as the Facilitator

It requires a tremendous amount of energy to design, build, and host retreats. I encourage you to think carefully about the immediate time before and after your retreat offerings as well as the month or two leading up to your event. I typically start my preparation for retreat leading thirty to forty days ahead of time. I pay careful attention to my sleep, my nutrition, my commitment of time, and my alcohol and caffeine intake. I try to get myself into a state of optimal functioning and optimal health before I travel to host retreats.

Consider having a support person or administrative assistant who can help you manage your retreat planning and registrations and who can ideally be there on-site to assist with group setup and guest management services and to take care of all the details so that you can focus exclusively on hosting.

Do as much planning ahead as you can. You can never be too prepared for hosting your retreat, but also while on-site, allow your group to do the work in your group sessions. Your attendees can get a lot out of a group session where you provide three to five journal prompts and allow them to write, reflect, and share. You don't need to prepare hours and hours of content or slide decks or lectures for your guests while on retreat. The most beautiful retreats allow guests to gain a deeper understanding of their own inner knowing and that comes from building in opportunities to think, process, and reflect.

Build in breaks for yourself. You do not have to go on every outing or excursion. It's perfectly OK to arrange for excursions that your guests can participate in while you give yourself time to rest and restore. One year, my group decided to go zip-lining and horseback riding for the day, and I stayed back at the property with my assistant and napped by the pool and got a massage. It was such a gift to allow myself this break midweek. My guests came back with big smiles and fun stories about their wild adventures, and I felt fully rested and replenished for the rest of the retreat work ahead of me.

Let your group know that when you're on, you're on and when you're off, you're off. This means that when you're in front of them leading sessions, you're fully present and engaged, but when you're off the clock, you're allowed to be enjoying your downtime too. Many times people will come up to you between sessions and want to ask you more questions or talk with you about their insights or discoveries. If you're open and available to that connection, then joyfully enter the conversation, but if you do not feel available to it, it's important to hold that boundary and simply let them know that you'd love to hear more about it at another time, but that you need quietude or rest at that moment.

You get to enjoy the retreat too. This means that you can attend yoga sessions, get a massage, go on excursions, or stay on the property and have a nap. You get to enjoy all the meals that are prepared for your group too, but it doesn't mean you have to eat with your group. There were times when I took my meal to my room or took my meal on the patio near the pool. Sometimes it's energizing to be with your retreat attendees, and sometimes you need space to breathe and recharge.

Clear your schedule three to five days before and after your retreat. If you can arrive before your guests and stay longer than them, then try to extend your stay to do that. Give yourself that gift of time to prepare and plan before your retreat and rest and recover after.

Learning How to Trust the Process

Sometimes things don't always go as planned while on retreat. I've faced almost every snafu you can imagine over the past twenty years from getting seriously ill while hosting in Costa Rica to a severe ice storm in northern Michigan for my winter reset retreat that almost prevented us from leaving the retreat center on the final day. I've also experienced guests who were very sick while on retreat; animals, scorpions, tarantulas, and giant beetles in guest rooms in Costa Rica; missed flights and connections; and times when all the months of planning leading up to the retreat felt like they went out the window.

It can be really challenging to be faced with unexpected issues when you're already feeling the responsibility of managing your retreat and you have guests looking to you for security and reassurance. But this is when your pre-retreat preparation work can be really beneficial. You can take a deep breath, reset your focus, stay present, and remain flexible and in flow.

"Trust the Process" is something my mentor used to tell me, and it comes in handy when hosting retreats. If you're willing to stay connected to whatever unfolds and allow it to teach you something or bring you a meaningful message, then nothing is wasted as you move through your entire retreat journey from beginning to end.

There are so many symbolic translations that can be very powerful learning opportunities for us. I believe when you are connected to the purpose and truth of what you've been called to create, then somehow everything that unfolds (whether planned or unplanned) is part of the divine order of that experience.

Retreats can be beautiful departures from our everyday lives. When on retreat, we get to expand our consciousness of who we are and who we want to become. New versions of ourselves can emerge and lost or hidden parts of ourselves can return. When we open up to the magic and mystery that retreat energy brings forth, miraculous outcomes occur.

CHAPTER 9

Creating Online Courses

Building an online course can be an excellent source of additional or passive income, and therapists have a wealth of knowledge to share when it comes to online course creation.

Courses can help us serve a larger audience and scale our income. When you invest the time it takes into creating an online course once, you'll be able to generate recurring revenue from it over and over again as long as you have an audience who wants your content and your course is still relevant, useful, and priced appropriately.

What Will You Teach?

When considering creating an online course, you need to think about teaching something that you love explaining, teaching, and sharing. What's one thing that you find yourself explaining a lot to your clients? What's one thing that helps your clients make major improvements to their lives? What's something that people always ask you about? Something that you might even feel is obvious to you, but might not be obvious to others?

Take a moment to brainstorm about what you could teach in your online course. Would it be skill building? A strategy? Is it psychoeducational? Is it a creative course or something that might help people maintain healthy habits? Is your course holistic or based on a wellness theme? Is it clinical? Do you break something complex down into something very easy for people to understand?

Building a Path to Course Completion

Once you've identified your course topic and you have that narrowed down, then you need to break that topic down into simple sequential steps. We usually build courses with an odd number of chapters or modules that our students can follow. Think about three, five, or seven steps for your course and consider what has to come first, second, third, and so on in order for your prospective student to move through your course material with ease and success.

Consider where your client is right now with their knowledge on this subject. And then consider where your client wants to be by the end of taking your course. How will you move them through that process? You're really taking your course students on a journey from step 1, where they are now, to step 5, where they want to be.

Next, take each of those steps or modules and consider the specific milestones, action items, and important information that your students must get from you for each of these modules to easily understand the topic.

Ultimately, we want our students to not only purchase our course but also finish the course too, and we want to help our students get the results they're looking for from taking our courses.

Understanding Your Ideal Student

We can build the most amazing course in the world, but if we don't really understand our ideal student and know what their problem area is and know what results they're looking for, it may never sell to anyone.

When you're building a course, you need to be crystal clear in identifying what the problem area is for your ideal student and how your course will help them get the results they're looking for. Consider all of the specific problems your ideal student might have.

How are they feeling now? Where are the gaps in their knowledge? What parts feel really hard or overwhelming to them? How can you break those things down into simple steps for your students? What do you think your ideal students need the most help with right now?

To take this a step further, we also want to understand more about our ideal student such as

- Their beliefs and values
- Their age range
- Any barriers to accessing information
- Socioeconomic status
- Education level
- Employment status
- Family/support system

In addition to general marketing demographics, we also want to understand their thoughts in purchasing your course. What objections or barriers might they have to taking your course? Why would they want to take this course now? Is it time sensitive? Does it feel affordable or valuable to your ideal customer?

Building Your Course Material

Once you've identified what you think you want your course to be about and who it's for, now it's time to map out your course material.

The best way to do this is to grab a bunch of Post-it Notes and start writing down every single idea, story, example, theory, exercise, and little bits of wisdom you will share throughout this course. A really good course has a combination of all of these things. Ideas, stories, theories, exercises, checklists for students, etc. Try to mix it up as you work on this step and include all of these types of materials for your course.

There are no bad ideas here. Just use this exercise as a brain dump. You can always edit and toss ideas out later. This is the time to get *all* these steps and ideas you have out of your head and onto paper.

I'll use the five-module course to describe the rest of this process, but of course you can have more or fewer modules in your online course.

Next, find a big clean empty floor space in your home and create your five modules on five Post-it Notes and stack them up in a vertical line from top to bottom.

Add a title to each module step for now so you're clear about what you're teaching in each section. You can refine those titles later, but it will help you frame up an outline as you do this next step.

Next to each module, go through every single Post-it Note idea you wrote down and assign them to one of your specific modules for your course. If you have leftover Post-it Notes that really don't belong to any specific module, you can edit these out or maybe consider adding them to a "bonus" section of your course.

Then, consider all the lists you might include for your students. These are the action items you want your students to take as they move through your course. Think checklists, bullet lists, to-do lists, or never-do lists that you could share inside your course related to what you're teaching.

You should have a very clear idea of what your course will include, how you will divide up the course material into specific modules, and what material you will include in each module. Now you should be ready to actually create your content.

Creating Content

Start by making a simple working document or workbook or slide deck for each module. Ideally, if you're making a workbook, this will have short explanations and workable space for your students to write and fill in sections.

Move through each Post-it Note idea under each module and start to develop these worksheets or slides. This will give you an excellent outline for you to record your video or audio lessons for each section of each module. Once you have done this step, review it very carefully from start to finish and make sure it makes sense moving in this order.

Then edit, edit, edit.

Once you've developed the resources for your course, ask yourself these questions:

- Will this material make sense to your prospective student?
- Does it move in order—step by step?

- Do you break up the information you're teaching with places for your student to work and make progress?
- Are you including simple checklists and action items for your students?
- Will your student feel like they're moving in a logical order from where they started to where they really want to be?
- Does your course help your students move from "problem" to "result"?

Recording Your Course Modules and Lessons

The easiest way to do this is by recording yourself on Zoom. You can share your screen and move through your course worksheets or slide deck as you teach the material. Keep your mouse over the "pause" button as you are recording. If you need to pause the video, you can easily click that button, take a break, and come back to recording in the same video segment. If you have a longer amount of time and a larger budget, you can of course also hire someone to edit your course videos.

Video Recording Tips

- Make sure you have great lighting and excellent sound quality.
- Keep your energy up.
- Look into the camera as you speak to your students and smile.
- Remember you can always delete and rerecord or edit your video—it's OK if you make mistakes.
- Shorter clips are much better than long video lessons.
- I recommend making your video lessons no longer than ten minutes for each segment you record.
- Start with a short "welcome" clip—congratulate your students for enrolling in this course, give them a quick overview of what you'll be teaching, and help them visualize their results and success from where they are now to where they'll be after they complete this course.

- End each video lesson with some encouragement for your students and give them a little teaser of what they'll learn in the next lesson to incentivize them to keep moving through the course material.

Our goal is to help students complete the course and get the results they were hoping for. A bonus would be that they love the course so much they recommend it to others.

Once you have all your Zoom recordings complete, download them onto your computer, then upload them onto a course hosting site or to your website.

You can also, of course, teach your course live and record it while you're teaching it for the first time, then sell the recordings. But if you do this, you will need signed consent from any attendees or students who might be seen or heard in the recording. You can simply have them sign something upon purchase of the live course that says, "By attending this live course, you agree that you allow us to record this course and that the recording may include your image, a video of you in the course, or your questions or interactions. If you do not agree to this, you can purchase the recording of the course and watch it after it's been taught live."

If the tech end of course building feels overwhelming to you, I suggest you consider hiring a virtual assistant (VA) or support person to assist you with this portion. You don't want this to become a barrier to your course being produced and out in the world serving your audience.

It's critical to know when it's helpful or vital to outsource aspects of your work as an entrepreneur. Consider doing the things that only you can do and allow your team to support you in other tasks so you are free to focus on only the portions you can create yourself.

Building Your Sales Page

Your sales page should include a few key components:

- A short and clear course title
- How long your course should take students to complete
- The problem your students might be experiencing (in their language) and how your course can solve that problem for them

- A breakdown of the modules you're teaching and how you teach this material (handouts, video or audio lessons, etc.)
- Info about why you're the perfect person to teach them this material (your expertise, authority, success story with what you're teaching, etc.)
- Testimonials from people you've taught this to before if you can include those
- The cost of the course
- When you offer it (is it open all the time or do you only open your course a few times a year?)
- Bonus offers if you're including those
- FAQs your students might have
- Why they should consider buying the course now and not later
- And, of course, a button or multiple call to action buttons where your ideal student can purchase your course

Sharing the Course with Your Audience

Now you need to share your completed course and sales page all over so your potential students will know it's available and hopefully purchase it from you.

You can share your course in the following places:

- Directly with your ideal students, clients, referral network, friends, family—whatever applies
- On your social media pages
- In your email newsletter
- On LinkedIn
- On all the "Marketing Monday" type posts in therapist groups on Facebook
- On your website
- Cross-promote across other websites (if applicable and possible)

Consider Affiliate Sales

You can encourage others to help you sell this course for an affiliate percentage bonus. When you create an affiliate link for colleagues, whenever someone purchases using their affiliate link, you will get the sale and your affiliate sales member will get a flat fee or percentage cut of your course sales—whatever you choose when you set it up.

Many online hosting sites such as Kajabi, Kartra, Teachable, Podia, and others make this easy to do inside their software. Many website hosting sites such as Weebly also have affiliate options.

Just remember, people need to see something about seven times before they really see it. One of the biggest mistakes I see when I do coaching with therapists is they build these amazing courses, they build the sales page, then they launch it to the world once and no one purchases it, and then they wonder what happened and end up feeling like a complete failure.

Part of what will make your course launch a success has to do with nurturing the audience in front of you with lots of free resources and value before you ever sell to them, and part of it has to do with how many times they see it.

Launches

Launches are not for the faint of heart. It is so hard when we put so much effort into something, we take the time to build it from scratch, we finish it and feel great about it, and then we put it out to the world and it doesn't convert like we thought it might.

Believe me, I've been there!

The first day is very exciting. People are buying it and you feel so incredible! Then the second and third day come and you wonder, Oh my gosh, what did I do? No one is buying this. Is this it? Am I only getting like five sales on this offer?

After you take some time to feel what you're feeling in a launch cycle, then it's time to put on your business strategy hat and learn more about what happened. We never fail or lose; we're just learning. Nothing is ever wasted. Your course can be repurposed or sold again and again. Maybe it was the timing of your sale? Maybe your audience isn't warm enough yet? Maybe they don't have enough trust in you or you haven't earned the authority you need to sell to them yet? Maybe they didn't see your offer because you only put it in front of them once or twice. Maybe your course isn't really answering the need they have right now? Maybe it was priced incorrectly? Maybe it wasn't enough information or maybe it was too much or too long as a course?

Whether your launch feels like a success or a failure, there are lots of ways we can learn from these experiences. If your launch was a huge success, then rinse and repeat it and offer something similar again. If it didn't perform well, it's time to go back to the drawing board and find out what went wrong.

The Selling Window

Sometimes having a specific window of opportunity to purchase the course helps. This means you have an open and closed cart date and remind your audience that they only have so many days before the course is closed and then they won't be able to access it.

Sometimes we want to have an open-ended course that is always available for purchase by our audience at any time of the year. There are pros and cons to each of these options. It sometimes depends on the size of your audience or whether you're offering something that might include a live component of coaching or support with each cohort that moves through a course.

Sometimes if they don't have any pressure to buy and your course is available anytime, then students might think, *I can come back and buy this later* and later turns into never. If you say the cart is closing on XYZ date, it can help people make a decision to purchase knowing it's time limited.

There is, however, something to be said for evergreen courses that are always available. You don't have to go through the roller-coaster effect of driving up all of your energy and marketing efforts to an open cart, holding your breath while the sale is going on, and then closing the cart, taking the course sale buttons down and wrapping it up until the next launch.

Lots to consider here, but ultimately you are the CEO of your business. You get to decide what works best for you, and you also have the freedom to pivot your plan if ever you feel like what you're trying isn't working the way you expected.

Remember that we cannot wait for the time to create our online course; we have to make the time to create our online course. I suggest you map out a strategic plan. Consider your timeline and be realistic. It could take you longer than you think to design, develop, record, build, and launch your first course. When I built my first online course on how to build a thriving practice, I spent time developing the outline and the workbooks first, then I took several days off work and batch recorded the entire course in a few days. This helped me a lot because starting and stopping the process would have been a choppy experience for me. I liked moving quickly through each module, and before I knew it, I was ready to build my sales page and open the cart to my very first launch.

My first launch was a five-figure launch for me because I had the key components in place. I had spent a lot of time nurturing my audience with tons of free value and resources, so they had time to build that "know, like, and trust" factor with me. I listened carefully to what they were really asking for from me, and I built things that answered their specific questions. I decided for my first few launches to do a closed cart, which seemed to help a lot. Rather than offering any early bird discounts or sale pricing, I offered bonuses instead. Bonus offers can incentivize people in a stronger way to purchase now while the bonus is included. After several launch cycles of the same course, I decided to keep it open and just offer it as an evergreen course. I probably sold less courses this way, but it was less of a time and energy investment for me too.

Instead of launching, I posted links to my course in my email signature, mentioned it in my newsletters and opt in to my email list, and dropped links to it in my Facebook community when appropriate. Sometimes I would make separate sales posts about the course too. But this method saved me the time and emotional cost of launch cycles and freed me up to focus on building my next courses, which I did five times over.

Lastly, you get to decide what you feel is best for you and your audience. Smart and savvy business owners are flexible and can pivot when necessary. Listen and observe the trends of your launches to determine how you want to shape the future of your online courses and passive income streams.

CHAPTER 10

Building a Group Practice

One of the biggest regrets I have being a psychotherapist and business owner is that I didn't build a group practice sooner. I never thought I could manage a group practice and I never even imagined how I would start one. But, for over a decade, I had completely booked out my practice with thirty-five clients a week (too many) and a long waitlist to be seen. I was overwhelmed every time a new referral inquiry came in. I had nowhere to put these clients and not a single slot left on my calendar for months.

Then COVID-19 hit and I was faced with an avalanche of requests to be seen for therapy. My already full caseload with a waitlist just exploded with high-need referrals, and it was like I was trying to drink from a fire hose. I was drowning in work, trying to make sense of the pandemic myself and support my kids through their own experiences while moving from a lifetime of in-person, brick-and-mortar practice to the whole new world of virtual therapy and telehealth appointments while trying to manage the growing demand for services.

Those were very, very difficult days for all of us.

Virtual sessions coupled with the fear and uncertainty of the pandemic exhausted me. I remember finishing seven sessions a day on a screen feeling the burn and strain behind my eyes and the pressure in my head. It was grueling at first and I longed for a break.

It was certainly not the ideal time to even entertain the idea of building a group practice, but I felt a desperate need to expand in order to meet the growing demand of waitlisted clients. Somehow I carved out enough time in the evenings and weekends to learn how to build a group practice. I miraculously found the most incredible therapist who was willing to slowly learn and grow into being part of my group practice, and the Thrive Advantage Group was born!

There are a lot of things to consider when building a group practice, and this chapter will walk you through all of the fundamentals.

Disclaimer: It is recommended that you work with your accountant and lawyer to be sure that the way you're structuring your group and how you're setting everything up is in accordance with the laws of your state or region. This information is meant to be a guide, but it's by no means a replacement for tax or legal advice.

Setting Up Your Group Practice as a New Business

If you take insurance in your solo practice, or if you are a cash-free practice, but you offer superbills, you'll want to be sure to apply for the NPI 2. An NPI 1 can be used for solo providers and an NPI 2 is used for group practices.

If you originally created a business under your name (such as I did when I built my solo practice as Megan Gunnell, LMSW, PLLC), then you'll want to consider opening your group practice as a second LLC or PLLC or forming a DBA (doing business as) under your original solo practice. Again, check with your accountant and attorney to be sure that this type of business structure works for your state or region.

But ultimately, when you're building a group practice, you are building a sellable asset. Therefore, it's important that you form your group practice with a name other than your first and last name. When you build and scale a business over the years, you may end up selling it, and it would be much easier and more appealing for someone else to purchase your group practice from you if it's listed under a company name that is not your first and last name.

You'll also want to be sure to contact your liability insurance provider and let them know you're building a group practice and you'll need to add group coverage to your plan. Each therapist who joins your team must also have proof of their own individual liability insurance coverage too. As the group practice owner, you must have group coverage on top of your own individual plans. If you're offering telehealth, you can also ask your insurance provider about additional coverage for cyber security and telehealth services.

Structuring Your New Hires—1099 or W2?

Some states do not allow you to hire 1099 independent contractors. They require you to structure your group practice with W2 employees, which means you will need to withhold their taxes, pay them payroll as employees, and potentially offer health insurance or other benefits.

If you are allowed to structure your team as 1099s, then each person would need to complete a W-9 form for you. Independent contractors are meant to work independently, meaning you cannot dictate what their hours will be. You cannot require mandatory staff meetings, and you cannot offer them annual bonuses. In addition, independent contractors are not supposed to work exclusively full-time for you and your group practice. If that's the case, it's best to structure your team as full-time W2 employees of your company. Independent contractors should have other sources of income and work for other people and places outside of your group practice.

With companies like Alma and Headway, it's easier than ever for therapists to build their own caseloads in private practice. And with so many offering telehealth sessions, many therapists who formerly might have had a barrier to entry into the world of building a private practice can now build a practice very easily.

That said, when hiring therapists to join your team, consider what your group practice can offer and help them understand the full value of being an important part of your group practice. For example, as the group practice owner, you're offering a trusted long-standing relationship with all of your referral sources to help keep your referral stream flowing and caseloads full. You're also offering marketing for the group practice, potentially someone on your team who does billing, bookkeeping, payroll, and credentialing, and you're either managing your website yourself or having someone on your team doing that as well.

In addition, you're providing training on how to onboard and manage seeing new clients and how to use your EHR system (such as Owl Practice, SimplePractice, or TherapyNotes). You might also be providing added support or guidance to your team members with regard to case consultation or practice management skills.

Many therapists do not want to do all of the back-end work of managing a practice. They do not want to be responsible for the billing, marketing, website management, credentialing, payroll, compliance, and general business management aspects of running a practice. Some therapists just want to focus on providing excellent clinical work and be part of a group practice where the owner of a group can take care of all the rest.

Where to Find a Qualified Candidate

You can create a job posting with the details of your position and post it in a variety of places such as Indeed and LinkedIn.

You can also use your network. Ask every therapist you know whether they know anyone who might be interested in joining your practice. Connect with local colleges and universities, especially in the spring when new grads are searching for job opportunities. You can list your position on virtual job boards, create hiring posts, and ask to have your info placed in a student email, newsletter, or digital bulletin.

Use the power and reach of Facebook groups. There are many Facebook groups for local therapists in your city or state. You can post your job posting in those groups and also in the larger national Facebook groups, such as the Thriving Therapists Facebook group, under the Marketing Monday threads each week.

Finally, blast out that you're searching for a therapist all across your own personal and business social media pages. Include the call to action to "share this post" and expand your reach. You never know, someone from your social media circles might know someone who could be the perfect fit for your next hire.

Interview Questions to Ask a Prospective New Therapist

Basic Overview Questions

1. Tell me about your background and experience thus far.
2. Why did you choose to become a therapist?
3. Why do you feel you might be a good fit for our group practice/agency?
4. Tell me about your strengths and weaknesses (personal/professional).
5. Have you ever been in therapy yourself? What was your experience like?
6. How would you describe the way you work best (self-starter, collaborator, independent, team player, leader, follower, etc.)?
7. What qualifications do you think might set you apart from other candidates?

Training and Experience Questions

1. Tell me about your educational training and any additional training or CEs you have completed or are interested in adding as you continue to learn as a therapist.
2. What population do you love working with the most?
3. What population would you not feel comfortable working with?
4. What's something that you're really looking forward to with regard to working in a group practice that you're not currently doing now?
5. Are you interested in staying in a group practice for a while or building your own solo practice as soon as possible?
6. How would you handle a client who has suicidal ideations or tendencies or a client who is a risk to self or others?

Personal Questions

1. Tell me a little bit about your personal life.
2. What do you enjoy doing in your free time?
3. How many hours a week would you ideally like to work?
4. What does your ideal schedule look like?

Collaboration Questions

1. What motivates you as a member of a team? What overwhelms or frustrates you?
2. How would you like us to connect (i.e., text, email, phone calls)?
3. How do you like to receive feedback?
4. Can you think of a past scenario that was positive or negative in working with a supervisor or boss? How did you handle that?

Thriving as a Therapist

1. What do you do for self-care?
2. Do you consider it easy or difficult to maintain healthy boundaries with your work-life balance?
3. Have you ever had to navigate a difficult situation with a client (in terms of transference or boundaries)?
4. How do you manage stress?
5. Where do you see yourself in five years?
6. Would you have any interest in speaking opportunities, workshops, group therapy programs, blogging or writing, or facilitating retreats for our team?
7. How can I best support you and your goals?
8. Do you have any questions for me?

If you're searching for another great resource to help you build a thriving group practice, be sure to check out Maureen Werrbach and The Group Practice Exchange (TGPE). The above list of interview questions was inspired by a resource from TGPE.

New Hire Checklist

Be sure to get all of these things from your new therapist:

- Completed W-9 form (if you structure your therapist as a 1099)
- Contract signed by therapist
- A signed Business Associate Agreement or BAA agreement (this operates like your business-to-business confidentiality agreement)
- A copy of their driver's license

- A copy of their degree
- A copy of their professional license
- Their NPI 1 number and EIN number
- A copy of their LLC registration
- A copy of their individual liability insurance
- Professional bio and headshot for your marketing materials
- Direct deposit banking info or payroll set up (Gusto or Square, for example)

Things to Review with Your New Hire

If you're offering telehealth, make sure your new hire has strong Wi-Fi, a router, and an excellent internet connection for virtual appointments.

Be sure they have a quiet, professional space in their home for telehealth appointments, and test your video calls with them prior to their first appointment to ensure that they have good lighting and sound and they know how to make good eye contact in a virtual session setting.

Let your therapists know that they can create a spreadsheet of their clients to track who they are seeing so that they can track payments and charges in addition to their EHR system if they want to do so. Next, you'll want to add them as a provider and train them on your EHR system. You can create a test client and practice scheduling, getting into the billing system, canceling an appointment, and testing the telehealth portal so your new therapist feels confident using the system.

New Therapists Orientation and Training Tips

Be sure to review what they can expect from working with your group, how you handle new clients, and your policies on no-shows, late cancellations, and confidentiality. You never want to assume that your new hire is familiar with how it works to do outpatient psychotherapy work. You may have a highly skilled candidate with a lot of clinical experience joining your team, but they may not understand the ins and outs of taking a new client from intake to termination in the outpatient mental health arena.

Be sure to give your new therapist plenty of room for questions and support. Practice using the telehealth portal together. Tell them how you handle it when a client is late for a session. How long do you wait for a client before you reach out or offer to reschedule? How do you handle late cancellations and no-show charges (i.e., when do you run those charges)? Do you have any exceptions to this policy (e.g., if the client or their family member is ill or if they have a personal or work emergency)? Do you give one grace for a missed appointment? Or charge the client the first time it happens?

The more you can invest in your onboarding, orientation, and training, the more time you'll save yourself later.

Ultimately, we open group practices to be able to serve more clients in need and to work smarter, not harder. Try to build a very independent team from the start. The more questions you answer early in the process, the more confidence your therapist will feel and the more freedom you'll experience as the group practice owner.

Be sure to review clinician-client confidentiality at the first appointment. I always train my therapists to use this language at the start of the first session with a new client.

> *"Before we get started I always like to go over two important practice policies. We do require twenty-four hours' notice to make any changes or cancel your appointment. If you happen to forget your session or cancel with less than twenty-four hours' notice, you would be billed your full session fee. Also, your confidentiality is really important to me and will never be jeopardized unless there is a risk of you hurting yourself or someone else."*

This quick reminder at the start of the first session helps clients understand that you have these two policies in place and helps them understand the boundaries of your work and what your expectations are for entering this working relationship as therapist and client.

I also like to explain that if I see a client in a public space, I will not acknowledge them to protect their confidentiality and privacy; however, if they initiate with me, of course I'm happy to respond. Reviewing these details helps your therapist know that they can set the tone and establish good professional boundaries from the start.

Take the time to explain how to start and end sessions on time and discuss when you reschedule clients and how you engage with and communicate with clients in between scheduled visits. And be sure to discuss how you handle high-risk cases as well as how you handle it when clients are asking for medication management or psychiatry referrals or referrals to other providers.

Be sure to also train your new therapist on how to do documentation and explain when you would like this to be done.

How to Manage the Workflow

It's helpful to have a shared system for your waitlist. We created a spreadsheet for adding new clients to our waitlist, and each therapist has access to this document so they can easily go to it, color-code which clients they're following up with, and schedule those or mark on the sheet if the client has found another provider.

This password-protected spreadsheet includes clients' names, contact information, what insurance they have, preferred time/day to be scheduled, summary of their needs, who they were referred by, and a space for the therapist's name who followed up to schedule this client.

This helps my team stay very independent. Whenever we have a few clients on the waitlist, we simply notify the entire team to go to the waitlist and schedule if they have availability and openings.

Annual Reviews and Evaluations for Your Team

Every year, it's a good idea to do annual reviews and ask your team members to complete a group practice evaluation so you can get a better idea of what they need most from you and how you can support their individual career growth and development.

One reason people leave group practices is because they don't feel supported by the owner. You can prevent this by staying on top of your team members' needs and encouraging their professional interests and work-life balance.

Every year, I send out a Google Forms survey to my team members and ask them these questions:

1. What are your top professional goals for this upcoming year?
2. How can I best support you in achieving your goals?
3. What do you like the best about working with our group?
4. What parts of working with our team could be improved and what are your suggestions for this improvement?
5. Are you happy with your caseload?
6. My ideal client to work with is . . .
7. What types of continuing education are you interested in for this year?
8. Anything else you'd like to share with us . . .

This survey has been an excellent way for me to understand what my team needs most from me as the group practice owner and helps my team members feel personally supported in their career goals and in building their ideal work situation.

Marketing Your Group Practice

When you add a new member to your team, change your work hours or location, or make a change to the insurances you accept, it's a good idea to let your referral network know about it. You can do this with a handwritten note, an email blast, a rack card drop-off, or a formal letter on letterhead (with more business cards tucked inside, of course).

When writing a letter to your referral network, remember that these are likely very busy professionals who may only have a minute to scan what you sent them, so be sure to make your letter easy to scan and structure it almost like a press release.

Here's a sample referral letter you can use as an example, using your letterhead for your group practice.

MEGAN GUNNELL

(Date)

Dear _____,

Your Group Practice Name Here—Now Accepting New Referrals

After being in solo practice for my entire career, I met the demand for outpatient mental health services and formed a group practice. I'm pleased to announce I've added _____ highly skilled clinicians to my team, and we are now accommodating new referrals.

We serve adults experiencing

- Anxiety
- Depression
- Mood Disorders
- PTSD
- Trauma
- Grief & Loss
- Substance Use
- Postpartum Anxiety or Depression
- Adjustment Disorders
- Relationship Problems
- Communication Issues
- Difficulty Coping
- Women's Health Issues

Treatment methods include

- ACT—Acceptance Commitment Therapy
- CBT—Cognitive Behavioral Therapy
- DBT—Dialectical Behavioral Therapy
- EMDR—Eye Movement Desensitization and Reprocessing
- Integrative
- Interpersonal
- Humanistic
- Mindfulness-Based
- Strength-Based
- Solution-Focused

All sessions are conducted via a HIPAA-compliant, secure **telehealth** platform.

We can accommodate session times **seven days a week** for daytime and evening appointments.

We accept (**list insurances**) **and private pay** and can provide clients with a superbill to submit for out-of-network benefits.

We are a solution-focused team of compassionate, experienced providers and look forward to providing impeccable care to your referrals.

Sincerely,

Your Name and Credentials
Title, Company
Website

Final Thoughts

Building a group practice can feel daunting and overwhelming. But you can do this. Just take it one step at a time, and before you know it, you'll have an amazing team of therapists who can serve more clients in need.

CHAPTER 11

Pivoting to Coaching

Many therapists make the decision to pivot to coaching. Some are looking to refine their audience or offers, some want to design goal-focused or results-driven packages for clients, and some want to offer sessions outside of their state lines and not be confined by their clinical licensure.

When therapists decide to build an arm of coaching in their business, it's a good idea to create a completely separate company. This would require that you file a business entity (like a new LLC, S corp, or PLLC, for example), get an EIN for that business, build a new website, set up a new email address, and establish your business bank accounts for this business (remember to create a business checking account and two savings accounts). Creating a completely new business entity and structure helps protect your clinical license as you build your nonclinical coaching offers.

Coaching is very different from clinical psychotherapy work. You could build coaching packages or individual sessions for clients or build workshops, retreats, or trainings under your coaching domain. Whereas clinical therapy addresses symptom management and treats a specific diagnosis, coaching work does not. Coaching work focuses on helping clients meet specific goals or work toward achieving specific results. It can be much more solution-focused and have more of a guided, educational, encouraging tone than our clinical psychotherapy work.

When deciding how to build or develop a coaching arm of your business, it's important that you have a well-defined niche and you really understand who you'll be working with and what their specific needs and problems are that your coaching work will help them address or resolve. Successful coaches have spent time drilling down to really understand this portion of the work before building any packages, setting prices, or building offers.

The Coaching Help Statement

Spend some time considering what your coaching could help your clients achieve or do. When we build a help statement for our business, it cannot be vague. Once you determine what type of coaching program you're building, it's much easier to narrow down your help statement.

Creating a help statement is a good exercise in knowing more about who you serve and how you work with them. Consider your ideal client and what they need the most help with, then fill in the blanks of this statement for better clarity:

I help (<u>description of your ideal client</u>) with/manage/process/work on (<u>problem area the client needs help with</u>) so that they can (<u>desired result from working with you</u>).

How would that statement sound for the type of coaching work you could offer?

What type of coaching are you considering offering? There are a lot of ways you can show up as a coach, and here are just a few examples: executive leadership coaching, business coaching, health and wellness coaching, couples coaching, parenting coaching, or life coaching.

Creating a strong help statement will make your coaching offers memorable and effective. The more specific you are, the more clear your ideal client will be about whether or not you might be the person to help them.

Attracting the Right Clients to Your Coaching Offer

Building a coaching business goes hand in hand with building a platform. For more on platform building, see chapter 14. Once you have a well-defined platform or audience to market to, it becomes much easier to meet the needs of those prospective clients in front of you with coaching packages, programs, offers, or services.

As always, it helps to offer lots of free, high-value content and resources to your community while you're trying to establish your reputation and authority as a potential coach. Then, when your prospective clients are seeking more support from you, you have already gained their trust, making it easier for them to decide to purchase individual sessions, group sessions, or coaching packages from you.

When I heard the call inside my Thriving Therapists community for more support, I decided to build a small group coaching package for ten therapists. I had never created a coaching program before, and I needed to learn quickly what worked and what didn't work. I offered it for a little less than $300 per person and ten people signed up. They got one individual coaching session with me and two group sessions. It was great for the group and a really solid learning opportunity for me as an early coach.

I was able to make $3,000 for these Zoom sessions and built lasting relationships with ten therapists who went on to purchase more coaching with me beyond that, buy my courses, and attend my retreats and summits.

From this group offer, I then went on to build 1:1 coaching sessions and six-week individual packages too. I created a coaching page on my website to explain who coaching was for, what problems we address, and what results coaching can provide. I then used an app called Calendly to create a simple self-scheduling link for a free twenty-minute discovery call to see whether coaching might be right for my prospective clients.

Discovery Calls

In the coaching world, it's common practice to offer free discovery calls. The investment in coaching can be higher than therapy, and the population you serve can be more niched down or specific. Your discovery call works both to help a prospective client understand whether you might be able to help them and to help you understand whether the caller might be a good fit for the type of coaching you do. There have been times when people have called me for a discovery call and I've referred them out to other coaches. Sometimes people are asking me to help them with something that is outside my area of expertise.

Nine times out of ten, discovery calls are a good fit and typically they convert to either an individual coaching session or coaching package. When someone schedules a discovery call with you, you can host these on the phone or on Zoom.

There are three main parts to a discovery call. First, you need to hear what the client's issues are. Find out as much as you can about where they are now and ask them what has worked for them and what has not worked. Then find out where they want to be. What are they hoping to achieve? Ideally, you'll be able to explain how working with you would help them build a bridge from where they are now to where they would like to be.

Then ask them whether they'd like to know how it works to do coaching with you. Never assume. When you ask someone this question, it helps them affirm that they're interested in knowing more about your coaching program or packages. Then explain what your coaching program involves, how long it is, what's included, and how much it costs.

When you let them know what the price is, just state the price and pause. It's respectful to allow your client to take time to digest all the information about what you just shared and understand the various pricing options if you have more than one. Also, our natural tendency is to fill the gaps of silence with more talking, which could then sound like we're trying to justify the cost of our program or package.

When we pause after the price, the client pauses too and considers the investment. They typically have more questions or sometimes want to clarify something about the coaching work. Some coaches want to finalize a sale on the discovery call, but that's never been my style. I operate from an abundant frame in all of the things I do, and something about trying to make someone pay for coaching right then and there feels pressured and like you're operating from a scarcity or predatory mindset and that is not how I operate in my business.

Instead, I let the client know that I will follow up the call with all of the information we reviewed and include self-scheduling links where they can schedule and pay for their coaching session or package. I also include a coaching contract for them to review and sign. The contract reviews the terms of our agreement, the details of the package, confidentiality and intellectual property rights, what happens if the client or I need to cancel for any reason, that this work is not psychotherapeutic in nature and that it is business coaching work meant to help therapists learn how to build and scale their business, and it, of course, includes all of the legalese my attorney included when they drafted this contract for me.

Investing in Your Business

This brings up a great point on investing in your business and the professionals who help you run your business. When I was first starting out, I thought the cost of paying for an accountant and an attorney was prohibitive. I was searching for shortcuts and ways to get around hiring these professionals, but soon I realized that these investments actually saved me a great deal of time and money and were worth every penny. My accountant guided me on when to move my business structure from a PLLC to an S corp and helped me understand all of my eligible deductions for my business. And my attorney-drafted documents such as my contracts and liability waivers that financially protected me when situations arose around cancellations or any client changes that were made to coaching packages or retreats, for example. While these investments can feel like a lot when you're just building various aspects of your business, they are wise investments to make that will help you feel protected and secure as a business owner.

Coaching Sessions and Packages

Once a coaching client reviews what I send them, they have time to consider whether or not they want to sign up for coaching sessions. At the time of this publication, my packages include live individual coaching calls on Zoom, unlimited email access, and a shared working Google Doc where we can work on outlining all of their ideas, offers, services, and what they're building, as well as a place to list the action items and homework they should try to accomplish between our live calls.

Coaching packages can be designed however you want. They can be one-off sessions, six-week packages, three- to six-month programs, or even longer time frames than that. I've seen many variations on these packages, and they can include Voxer, WhatsApp, or email access to you, or you might include Loom videos or trainings for them in addition to live coaching call support.

And the nice thing is you also get to adapt and change your package over time to meet the needs of what your clients require the most help with. You can also adjust your pricing too. It takes a few sessions and a few clients to sort out what feels long enough and what feels like the right price for what you're offering to them.

You can justify higher prices for coaching work in comparison to therapy pricing because the work is very goal-directed and shorter in duration than therapy. Some coaching sessions can provide clients with the results they're looking for in one session. Some can complete their work in six to twelve weeks. But when a person enters into therapy, it's typically for an undefined, much longer period of time and what you're working on is very different from what you would work on in a coaching relationship.

Benefits of Coaching

Therapists who build a coaching business quickly find that the work is exciting and energizing. It's fast-moving, usually short-term work and provides impressive results for your clients. In addition, you can earn more money per hour as a coach than you can as a therapist, freeing up more time to do the things you love doing.

When I started my coaching business and still had several days a week of therapy work too, I felt a physical difference in my body on the days I was doing coaching work vs. the days I was doing psychotherapy sessions. The clients you work with in coaching sessions are also feeling really good that they're making quick progress toward their defined goals. The feedback loop and positive energy from client to coach and from coach to client are truly palpable.

Therapists are well qualified to provide coaching services. We have more training and knowledge on human behavior than almost any other field or industry out there. We know how to structure a session, we can interpret resistance and blocks that our clients might be experiencing, and we're highly skilled in providing validation, compassion, and support.

I hope this chapter inspires you to think outside the box and consider how adding elements of coaching to your work could help you increase your impact and income.

CHAPTER 12

Speaking Gigs

A great way to diversify your income and increase your authority is to do public speaking. Building a speaking arm of your business takes some patience and effort, but with the right steps, you can easily leverage your expertise and secure paid keynote speaking opportunities.

The best way to begin building a speaking track of your business is to narrow down your signature talk. What is something you feel you could talk about for thirty minutes to an hour without any preparation right now? What's something that people ask you about all the time or something you feel you have a solid level of expertise around?

Do you specialize in something like self-care and mindfulness, trauma-informed care, couples communication, sexual health, grief and loss, coping strategies, or parenting, for example? What are the top ten things you could talk about in a one-hour presentation on your area of specialty or expertise? What's your hook? What's the juicy opening story to your talk? What's the major takeaway you're hoping your audience will gain from hearing your presentation?

That is your outline for your signature talk.

Great public speakers have a way of connecting with their audience. They include stories or vignettes that draw the listener in. They take listeners on a journey and make what they're sharing simple to follow and easy to remember. They know when to pause and when to repeat something.

Repetition is king! It's OK to repeat important aspects of your presentation so listeners really absorb the foundational message you're trying to convey.

Great speakers also know when to pivot if they're losing their audience's attention. These aspects of public speaking take time to develop. But these are good tips to keep in mind as you're building your presentations.

Slide decks should be simple too. Less is more when it comes to building a slide deck. If you put too many details on a slide, the audience will have trouble listening to you and reading what you wrote. Many times I see excellent presenters make this mistake. They have so much wisdom to share and end up having way too much information on each slide. Narrow down what you're sharing into simple, bite-size summaries. A solid slide deck should support the speaker, not distract the audience away from the presentation.

Building a Speaking Career

Organizations, clubs, local and national groups, summits, and conferences are searching for speakers. It's your job to make it known that you can present and make it easy for conference organizers or club and organizational leaders to hire you. When I first started out with my public speaking career, I was still working as a music therapist. I pitched to every place I could think of and offered to present for free. In exchange for the free talk, I would ask them for testimonials, photos, video clips, and introductions to other leads who might be looking for speakers like me.

I spoke as a guest lecturer at every university that would accept me. I simply emailed professors and asked them whether they wanted or needed a guest expert on music therapy. I submitted proposals to speak at medical conferences and music and creative arts therapy conferences. I spoke at churches, women's groups and clubs, Rotary Club, hospice conferences, nursing conferences, and schools. I booked as many talks as I possibly could to build my repertoire and expertise as a speaker.

Pitching to Speak

When you pitch to be a speaker for a club or organization, you can simply cold contact the director, connect with them on LinkedIn, email them, or call and ask them whether they might be interested in having a guest speaker present to their organization on the topic that you consider your specialty. If you're pitching to people in this way, it's also helpful if you have your signature talk title and short description written up, a short bio, a headshot, a list of places you've presented, and any testimonials you might have from those presentations.

Sometimes directors of organizations will inquire about your rate or speaker fee, but if they don't ask, you can always ask whether they offer an honorarium. I probably presented thirty to forty times for free before I started charging for my talks. Then over time, as my speaking career really started to take off, conference organizers were emailing me asking me to be a paid keynote for their conferences.

If you're interested in speaking at conferences, you can google "call for proposals" followed by the type of conference you're interested in speaking at. For example, you could google "call for proposals women's conferences" or "call for proposals medical conferences" and you will find your way to submitting a proposal to present.

The application process varies a lot, so pay careful attention to the details. Sometimes they want you to submit your CV and fill out information for CE (continuing education credit) approval, and sometimes they want a video clip of you presenting somewhere else (which is why when you speak for free, it's a good idea to ask whether you can get someone to take video clips and photos for you, or set up a tripod with your phone and record yourself). Some ask for speaker references, so keep your contacts from past speaking gigs in a place you can easily access them and ask every past contact you've presented for whether it's OK to add them to your reference list.

Be sure to read the fine print on conference applications. Sometimes even if they select you to be a speaker, you still need to pay to attend the conference. Sometimes you can negotiate a better rate on conference admission or even overnight accommodations in lieu of being a paid speaker. It never hurts to inquire.

Remember, you're building your speaker résumé and you're investing in your future potential to earn more as a public speaker. You know the saying "Sometimes you have to invest money to make money."

When I was building my speaking career, I applied to speak at conferences all across the United States and paid to fly myself to those stages. I knew I was investing in my authority as a speaker, and each time I did a speaking gig, I arranged to get photos, videos, and more testimonials. Many times I was invited back again year after year and moved up to larger size audiences every time I presented.

Writing a Speaker Bio

Your bio should be a short paragraph written in third person that summarizes who you are and gives an overview of your major accomplishments. Write your bio the way you would imagine someone introducing you then edit, edit, edit!

Most bios are twice as long as they should be. Your bio should be easy to read and be an overview of just the major highlights of your career. You do not need to name every place you've worked at or every single training or certificate you've acquired in your bio. Focus on the mission of your work and mention something that helps people understand why you're an expert in this subject matter. At the end of your bio, it's OK to share something clever and personal. Don't just say "She likes to garden in her free time"; say something more interesting like "In her free time, you'll find her digging in the dirt and creating stunning arrangements with fresh-cut dahlias." It's fun to close your bio with something unique about yourself in that last line—something that feels relatable and conversational.

Building a Speaking Page

Once you get going with your speaking gigs, it's time to make a speaking page on your website. Your speaker page functions like a speaking career résumé. It includes a photo and video library of your talks, a place for testimonials from past audience members or people who have hired you to present, and a clear call to action where people can book you to be a speaker for their event. You can even create a "sizzle reel" with several clips of your various presentations edited back to back in one video to showcase your best nuggets from your best talks and demonstrate the way you present to your audiences.

Your speaker page can list several titles and short descriptions of all of the talks you've given. It can also list the names or places where you've presented. If you get permission to use the organizations' logos where you've been a speaker before, then you can include those as well.

Adding a speaker page to your website is great when people are searching for a speaker on your topic, but it's also a great link you can share when you're pitching to present. It adds an instant layer of legitimacy, authority, and expertise.

Building Your Own Event

Many people looking to branch out into speaking end up building and hosting their own event as a way to capture photos, videos, and a marketing angle for their speaking page on their website. After speaking at the Bryant University Women's Summit in Rhode Island several years in a row, a lot of people came up to me and said, "What's your company?" I didn't have a company at the time. I was just "Megan Gunnell, LMSW, PLLC" for my solo private practice. I didn't have a company name or a brand or anything to share outside of my first and last name.

I went home after the third time I spoke at that conference and thought, *Maybe it's time to develop a brand—something larger than me, a company identity that I can share beyond my solo practice.* That is when the Thriving Well Institute, LLC was born. Originally, I built this company as an extension of my solo practice, speaking gigs, and retreat work for clients. When I developed the brand, I decided to host a company launch event.

I invited speakers who could speak on the subject of thriving in various areas of our lives (from medical to financial, etc.), and I asked them to prepare twenty- to thirty-minute TEDx-style talks. I prepared the opening talk myself on the concept of thriving and introduced this new venture to a sold-out audience of one hundred guests. We had vendors where guests could shop for self-care and thriving products, the four keynote speakers, professional photography, gift bags for all guests and raffle items, and we closed with a rooftop prosecco toast and light appetizers.

It was a huge success! I got sponsors to help offset the cost and sold tickets to the event. I cross-promoted it with the three other speakers and we sold out easily. Everyone who attended really enjoyed it, and I got great professional photos that I still use to this day for my company.

There are a lot of details to consider when hosting your own event, like taking out event liability insurance, hiring security or whatever is required from the venue if you serve alcohol, securing and negotiating the venue contract, integrating payment systems to sell tickets, marketing the event with enough notice to successfully fill it, and drafting any disclaimers or waivers guests need to check off and sign when they submit payment to attend.

But with enough time to plan and enough support, anything is possible!

Hosting your own event gives an instant boost to your authority, and it's a great way to build community, share your wisdom, test your signature talk, and create a follow-up offer for your audience too (such as a group mentoring or coaching session, a retreat or workshop, a membership, or even 1:1 coaching sessions).

How to Price Your Talk

Talking about money isn't easy for therapists. Here are some tips and tricks to help you navigate the discussion on what to charge for your talks. If you're pitching to speak, it's usually implied that you will speak for free. However, it's OK to ask "Is there an honorarium available for this presentation or another way I could help offset my costs to present?" If the talk does not include pay, you can ask whether it's OK to pitch your services at the end of your presentation and always be sure to get something out of a free talk (as mentioned above, such as photos, videos, or leads to other contacts who might want to book you for a talk, as well as testimonials and references you can share to help you secure future talks).

Things to Consider When Calculating Your Price Point for a Presentation

- Is the presentation in person or virtual?
- If in person, how far would you need to travel to speak?
- Does this include overnight accommodations, flight, rental car, etc.?
- How large is the audience?
- Do they have sponsors who might offset your speaker fee?
- How long will you be speaking?
- Will they want to record your presentation and use it again in the future? If so, how will you be paid for that use?
- Do they want anything before or after your talk such as any planning or prep meetings with you and their team or any follow-up consulting, training, or coaching sessions after you present?
- How long have you been a speaker and how much experience do you have?
- Is there room to negotiate the speaker fee or any of the extras such as travel expenses?
- Will they waive your conference registration fee if they cannot pay you to present but you want to attend the rest of the conference?
- Are you required to submit continuing education information for CE approval?

Things to Keep in Mind When Quoting Your Fees

- Your speaker fee should be two to three times higher than your hourly wage.
- Always start higher than you think they will accept. You only have one chance to get the highest amount for your presentation. They can always negotiate down, but they'll never offer more.
- If the speaker fee is lower than you hoped for, ask whether they're willing to collaborate with you on other ways you can monetize your time for being there such as adding on a masterclass session

with you for a fee to attendees or an additional workshop or training for an extra charge if possible.

- Many times if you're presenting locally and it's a live talk (not virtual), it requires you to block off several hours of your time to prepare, travel to the destination for the talk, give the talk, speak with people afterward, and travel back home. Consider all of the time this will take the day of the event, as well as all of the preparation time it will require of you to design and build this talk.

- The price you quote to the organization should scare you a little. If it doesn't, it's not high enough. What's the worst that can happen? They say that it's out of their budget, but will you accept something lower? They're not going to not invite you to be a speaker because your initial quote was too high. If anything, they may feel the opposite and have a new perception of your value when they hear your initial quote!

- Leverage your platform. If you have a sizable audience, use that information to secure a higher price for your talk. You can offer to share their conference, summit, or workshop with your audience (if applicable) in exchange for that higher price point for your quote.

- Take that one step further and ask them for your own affiliate link to their event that you can share with your audience. If you accept a lower price point for your talk, you can also request additional pay if you help sell out their event by promoting it to your audience. They will be able to track those registrations from your specific affiliate link.

Lastly, you're a highly skilled therapist with a wealth of knowledge, experience, and expertise to share with audiences across the globe. Promise me you won't undersell yourself. You're worth every penny. Aim high and see what happens.

CHAPTER 13

Outsourcing and Hiring a Team

As the momentum in your business picks up and you really begin to scale and have additional streams of income, you'll need to consider hiring support. No successful CEO expands without a team. But again, in our graduate degrees, no one teaches us how to do this. When I first considered adding team members to my business, I felt a lot of resistance. I was so used to operating as a lone wolf, as a solo independent psychotherapist, as the visionary entrepreneur of my own company that I did not want to allow others to help me at first.

I had control issues, trust issues, and always thought it was "just faster and easier" to do it myself. Pay attention to where your core wounds show up in your professional roles. These interpersonal issues show up for me over and over again as a CEO, and as much as I'm always continuing to work on these wounds in my personal therapy work, I'm also aware of the opportunities to heal them in my professional life too. If you have abandonment issues like I do, you might worry that if you give your employees too much work, then they'll leave you, or if you don't give them enough work, they'll also leave you.

Paying attention to your inner wounds and core family of origin stories and noticing how they show up for you as a leader and entrepreneurial business owner will help you shift how you manage your business and how you interact with your team members too. Once I recognized this was my fear, I was able to address it within myself, and it helped me make positive changes in the way I run my companies and engage with my team members.

How Do I Know It's Time to Hire Support?

If you're asking this question, it's time. Even early on, business owners could benefit from outsourcing small, part-time roles to others who can do some of their business tasks either faster, more efficiently, or better than they can. When I was considering hiring a VA, I kept questioning whether I really needed support. I was trying to make graphics for my business inside Canva, and I was absolutely terrible at it. I could do it, but it took me hours and hours to create one simple Facebook event cover image and it never looked the way I wanted it to. I felt like pulling my hair out sitting there trying to drag and drop images into a template and then realizing the whole thing just looked like a preschooler made it, rather than a professional, beautiful graphic I envisioned having that was aligned with my branding and corporate identity.

I thought, *If I could just have someone help me make things on Canva, that would be amazing.* Then as I was developing online courses, I wanted to take my workbooks and make them look beautiful and professional too. But there was no way I was going to take a twenty-page Google Doc and turn it into a full-color handbook overnight when I could barely even make one image work for me inside Canva.

I started considering how I wanted to spend my time as the leader of my company.

This is when I decided to interview and hire my first VA. I scheduled a Zoom interview with her and asked to see some samples of her work. I also wanted to know who her other clients were so I could look at some of the things she had done for them. Remember, I admitted having a high need for control and low trust, but in this case, when you hire slow, fire fast, you do yourself a tremendous favor in the long run.

Take your time hiring and make sure that every team member is aligned with your company mission and vision.

In addition to that alignment, you also want to feel like you have a free and easy, friendly flow with your team members. If your interactions in an interview feel off or awkward, keep interviewing. I remember hearing the CEO of Rent the Runway speak at a women's summit I was also a speaker at several years ago. She talked about building up this incredibly successful company and some of her best tips as a leader. One thing that really stayed with me was her advice around "hiring people who you'd love to spend a day at the beach with." She said everyone who applies is highly skilled and highly qualified. They all have solid résumés and experience, and on paper, they'd all be great candidates for the job. But when she interviews them, she asks herself, "Would I want to spend a day at the beach with this person?" And that wisdom has served me well.

I now have team members who are 100 percent behind supporting the vision I'm creating. They initiate ideas before I even think of asking them to take on a task, and I'd honestly travel with any of them anytime!

When I was in the Meta Facebook Community Accelerator award program for 2022–2023, we had four months of executive coaching and support from a huge team of incredible coaches and industry leaders. It helped me reshape the way I operate as a leader and how I manage my companies. From this program, I met my incredible marketing coach, Brittany Long, who asked me to do one simple exercise that dramatically changed the way I manage my time as a CEO.

She told me to take a sheet of paper and draw a line down the middle. Then make a list of all of the things someone else could do for me on one side of the paper and on the other side make a list of only the things that I alone can do for my business. This was so eye-opening! I started becoming aware of how much time I could invest in innovating and creating, writing, leading, teaching, facilitating workshops, and developing programs and in-person events, rather than all the hours I was wasting doing things in my business that I wasn't very good at, like creating Canva designs and bookkeeping.

Outsource what you can, and if at first you can only afford a few hours of part-time support, that's OK. Those few hours will return to you threefold, and as you begin to let go of the tasks that you don't need to be doing yourself, you'll discover how much space and freedom you have to continue being the innovative and visionary leader that you are and really want to be.

What Can a VA Do for You?

I get this question so often, I decided to make a simple list. Of course, a VA can also do many other things for you too, but here's a short list to get your wheels turning:

- Helping with graphic design/Canva
- Uploading content to YouTube
- Managing your emails (screen, respond, schedule for you, follow up and manage your email list)
- Creating a landing page
- Integrating payment systems into your sales pages/landing pages
- Tracking info/data management
- Managing social media platforms (creating content, posting, and engaging)
- Copywriting
- Blogging (uploading, finding copyright-free images, sharing blog posts for you on social media business pages, etc.)
- Completing general research such as comparative analysis; researching competitive pricing on things you might be purchasing for your business; narrowing a search for hosting retreats; sourcing facilities for trainings, conferences, or summits you might host, etc.
- Pitching you to a podcast or conference for a speaking engagement
- Inquiring on your behalf about opportunities to present, speak, network, and meet referral sources
- Updating your website (posting, updating)
- Managing payroll for your group practice
- Billing and bookkeeping

- Video editing and posting
- Podcast editing and posting
- Completing personal assistant-type tasks such as making travel arrangements, purchasing/shipping gifts, sending out referral letters, writing thank-you notes, etc.
- Helping you stay organized with productivity apps such as Asana or Trello

How to Structure Your New Hire

Most part-time contract workers will be set up as 1099 independent contractors, but always refer to your state laws and get accounting and legal advice before setting up anything related to your company structure.

Sometimes a VA or business manager that you hire runs their own company for their services and will have a contract for you to sign when you agree to work together. It's a good idea for you to also have a 1099 independent contract agreement on your end as well that outlines things such as the terms of your agreement, the background and purpose of your contract, scope of services, their rate of pay and when they'll be paid, how both parties should notify one another of termination of services, any confidentiality agreement between businesses, the protection of your intellectual property, and any other specific contractual details you need to establish.

I also have all team members sign a BAA, or a business associate agreement. A BAA establishes a legally-binding relationship between HIPAA-covered entities and any other business associates to ensure the protection of any protected health information, or PHI.

Managing Your Team

When I hired my first admin assistant, I didn't understand the importance of my leadership and how critical it is to have clear communication with my team members. I made a lot of assumptions that this person would know what I wanted them to do and not need much guidance from me. I also didn't feel like I could afford to pay this person what they deserved, so I made the mistake of trying to offer them support, guidance, and access to my resources for free in exchange for some of their time and work for me.

Don't make the same mistakes I did.

Be sure to clearly define the job description and role of your team member. Agree on an hourly wage and do not barter or trade for support. You should also plan to meet with them on a weekly basis and provide clarity around your expectations of both the work you're expecting support around as well as the timeline you expect it completed. After moving through two admin assistants early on, I hired my third assistant whom I promoted to business manager quite quickly.

I learned a great deal from my first two admin relationships and now feel like a much stronger and more effective leader with much healthier boundaries and solid communication with my team members. I would say anyone who is working for me now feels clear on what is expected of them in their role; they feel appreciated as a valued member of my team and well supported in their own growth and development within my organization too.

I learned that it's best to provide more training and orientation than you think you need and always leave room for questions from your team members. One of the best things I've ever done as a team leader is to ask every team member what their thoughts are on our upcoming projects, company goals, big dreams and ideas, as well as their thoughts on how to best approach the work at hand. This not only creates a great sense of investment and mutual respect inside your organization, but oftentimes when I ask for this type of feedback and collaboration, my team members will suggest more efficient ways of doing things that I never thought of.

I prefer to lead from a place of deep respect, admiration, and gratitude. No one likes to be told what to do, feel rushed to get it done, and feel unrecognized for their contributions. I try hard to ask my team members whether they can help me with something, give them plenty of time to accomplish the task without feeling pressured or hurried, and make sure to thank them for their support and collaboration.

Model Integrity in Your Leadership

Be the first to admit your mistakes and errors, and take accountability when something in your company goes wrong. I never assume when a team member makes a mistake that it's their fault. I try to ask myself how I am accountable because, ultimately, I'm the leader of my organization. Did I not provide enough clarity or training on something? Did I not check something that was mine to review? Did I not provide enough explanation or details when I asked for this task to be completed? How could I have been more clear?

When there are any errors in your company due to a mistake one of your team members made, model high integrity and accountability and take on as much responsibility as you can for the issue at hand. Ask your team members what they need from you and ask where they feel things fell apart or what happened from their perspective. Listen without judgment and validate compassionately. Be swift to apologize for any parts that are yours and work together to solve any issue or clarify things so the same mistakes do not happen again.

When your team members really knock it out of the park and excel in their roles, celebrate those victories with them. Increase their pay on a regular basis, remember their birthdays and work anniversaries, and give them annual promotions where appropriate. When you invest in your team, they feel invested in you!

And contrary to my fears that if I give my team members more work they will leave me, they actually see it as job security, and as their workload increases, so does our company growth and monetary gains across the board. When the company does well, we all benefit, and their income increases along with mine.

How to Best Support Your Team

I always want to know how I can best support their personal and professional goals too, and I offer annual evaluation forms to get their feedback on this. In my annual evaluation, I want to know whether working with my company helps them feel supported and in alignment with their goals. I also want to know whether they think there is anything I can do to make their job easier or better or whether there are things they want to expand into that I could help support.

For example, with my group practice team members, I always want to know whether the therapists who work for our group have any interest in blogging or doing speaking engagements or whether they'd like to run a group or host a one-day workshop or retreat, and if so, how can I help them achieve those goals.

Another example: my business manager is also a yoga instructor, and every time I run an international retreat, she offers our yoga sessions because it's in alignment with her passion and interest to facilitate yoga classes on retreats.

If there is something that your team members want to do, find out how you can best support them. Ask them what they think about your business development ideas and listen deeply to their suggestions on how to do things more efficiently. They're on the front lines doing the work that makes your company run smoothly. You probably don't know the ins and outs of what their roles entail. Be sure that you have regular and clear communication around your expectations and never function from assumption.

Ultimately, outsourcing and building a solid team is another way we can thrive as leaders of our organization. If you think you can just keep doing everything yourself, you might find yourself burned out and exhausted as you scale your business. Working with a dedicated team is a rewarding and healthy challenge. I'm always learning something new as I develop better ways of growing and expanding my team and business, and the mentorship and support I get to provide is richly rewarding interpersonally too.

Allow yourself to consider all the ways outsourcing and hiring team members can help you continue to build, expand, and scale your business to new heights. You'll never know until you try.

CHAPTER 14

Building a Platform

When entrepreneurs develop additional streams of income such as a coaching arm of their business, online courses, retreats, trainings, or workshops, for example, typically the level of success in selling these is directly tied to the strength of their platform. Notice I didn't say "size" of their platform. You can be very successful increasing your impact and income with a small, but well-developed platform. You do not necessarily need an audience of thousands to start monetizing offers, programs, products, and services, but what helps is if you have invested some time and energy into nurturing the audience or platform you do have in front of you by generously sharing resources and value with your platform so they can start to "know, like and trust" you as an authority and leader in your area of expertise.

What Is a Platform?

A platform is your audience. It's where people go or gather to learn more from you as a leader. It can be developed in a variety of ways. My two favorite ways to get started building your platform are by building a Facebook group or building an email list. It's best to try to do both simultaneously. Of course, there are other social media platforms where you could develop a following, but I've found that Facebook groups provide an opportunity for people to connect with one another, ask questions and answer posts inside the group, and provide support to one another. In these groups, you can easily organize resources and information for your group members, which in turn helps establish your authority, expertise, and value as a leader.

Identifying Your Ideal Client/Consumer/Customer

Before you dive into building your platform, it's important that you get super clear on who your ideal client is. Spend some time now defining all the details you can possibly think of about your ideal client. Who are they? What are their defining qualities? What are their values, beliefs, and motivating factors? What are their objections and limiting beliefs? What problems do they have? How might they be feeling about these problems? What do you think they would say about how to solve their main pain point or problem area? What gets in the way of their success?

Once you drill down and really understand more about your ideal client, then you'll have a better idea of how to attract them to your platform or email list.

Building an Email List

Direct email marketing is still the best when it comes to sales conversions. If you nurture your email list, create a solid funnel to add emails to it, and never abuse your email subscribers (meaning don't email them too much or spam them, etc.), then you'll always have your own warm audience to share your offers with.

You can create a lead magnet or opt-in on your website, which is a high-value resource, video, or training, for example, that people get in exchange for giving you their email address. There are lots of ways to automate this where the person enters their name and email into a form on a landing page from an email provider like Mailchimp or MailerLite, then the person automatically gets a copy of your freebie, and at the same time, they are automatically added to your email list. Great lead magnets or opt-ins can be a "how to" guide, a checklist, a worksheet, some type of "done-for-you" content, an educational resource, a road map to help shorten a process for your audience, a step-by-step guide, or any other type of valuable resource. People are typically looking for ways to save time, energy, or money. If your lead magnet can help them with one of those areas, they're more likely to give you their email in exchange for what you're offering them.

Another way to collect emails is to ask new members for their email address when they join your private Facebook group. These can be manually added to your email list at first, and then as you get more and more people joining your group, I recommend you consider using an app such as Group Collector to automatically load these email addresses directly into your email provider. Group Collector still gives you the option to manually approve or decline the member who leaves their email when they're trying to join your Facebook group, but once you approve that new member request, the email gets lifted out of the pending member query and added to a spreadsheet, and from there it gets automatically added to your email service provider and like magic, that new person is now on your email list!

Welcome Email Series

As you're building your email list and new members get added, it's a great idea to set up an automation to welcome your new members. This can be a single email or it can be a series of emails that go out to your new subscribers every day or every other day or even once a week for a period of time. Sending emails every day to a new subscriber feels too often for me personally. I opt to send out a welcome series of five emails that go out to any new subscriber on my list every couple of days from the starting point of entering my list.

These welcome emails begin with a warm welcome that reminds them how they signed up for my list. I thank them for being a subscriber and explain a little about my work, who I am, and the mission of my Facebook community and company. I also mention in the first email that over the next few days I will be explaining more about some of the various ways my programs, products, and services might help them. My subsequent emails go on to describe more about my work as an international retreat leader and how they can learn how to host retreats too. I also use this welcome series to discuss my courses and coaching and the benefits of working with me.

The goal is to help your new subscriber get to know you and your services and build an email newsletter that makes them want to open your emails. You want to strike a nice balance of sharing value and resources and letting them know you have other products, services, or offers they can purchase without feeling spammy or overly salesy. You can have a clear call to action in your email signature with links back to your resources or things you've built that clients can purchase. This way, even in emails you send that do not have a sales pitch, your links to offers will be embedded in your email signature or footer in case they want more from you.

How to Nurture Your List

Remember the 80/20 rule. You should be nurturing your audience 80 percent of the time and only selling 20 percent of the time. If you tip this too far toward selling, people will unsubscribe. You only have one chance to get someone onto your email list. You want to honor and respect that people have given you the chance to email them directly and not ruin this opportunity.

With any aspect of platform building, consistency is key. Plan to email your list (after your welcome series) about once a week or once every other week. Any more than that and it can feel like too much, and any less than that, people will likely forget who you are or what you're offering. That said, when you're launching a new offer, you might be emailing more frequently than once a week. You can explain this to your audience, and you can also allow them to opt out of the launch campaign if you set that up inside your email system.

Be sure to provide value to your email list. What do they want the most from you? Helpful tips? Shortcuts to save them time? Links to resources? Short videos from you with teachable topics inside? Does your list want encouragement, ideas, or ways to increase their income or reach? Do they need support or education from you? Consider again who your ideal client or email subscriber is and consider what they want and need from you the most.

You'll start to really understand more about your email list as you begin studying the insights and stats from your email campaigns.

Email platforms such as Mailchimp allow you to review a lot of details and data about your email list. You can find out exactly who opened your email, how many times they opened it, and even where they clicked on the links you included. You can learn a lot about how to improve your next email campaign by learning from the one you just sent to your audience. Mailchimp can even identify the optimal time to send your email campaign based on when your subscribers are most likely to open it.

How to Structure Your Emails

When drafting an email, cut out the fluff. Get straight to the meat of what you're writing about. Consider adding a compelling subject line. This is your main hook. It's what entices people to either open the email, skim over it, leave it unopened, delete without reading it, or worse, report it as spam.

The body of your email should be easy to skim. Consider breaking up longer paragraphs, and write the way you speak. For easy scanning for readers, use bullet lists and bold a few words or sentences that you want to highlight for them. Do not include too many embedded links or your email could be flagged as spam or sent automatically to the promotions tab. Same with photos. Only use a few photos. Using too many can send your email to a subscriber's spam folder.

Make good use of your email signature. Always include a clickable link back to your website or wherever you want to drive traffic to (e.g., back to your Facebook group, to the offer you're trying to sell, or to a link to sign up for a time on your calendar if that's what you're hoping readers will do).

It's helpful to include a PS section under your email signature where readers who quickly scan to the bottom can see what the final, quick call to action is. I find that the most clicks happen from the PS section of my emails.

Building a Private Facebook Group

I recognize my own bias as I write this section of this book. Building the Thriving Therapists Facebook group completely changed my life in just three short years. Creating this platform has allowed me to serve a much larger audience, make a bigger impact, and increase my income. As a result of building Thriving Therapists, I built five additional streams of income and completely changed the way I worked and lived as an entrepreneur.

Because of my Facebook group, I was honored to be one of thirty-three Facebook admins in all of North America to be selected for the Meta Facebook Community Accelerator Program 2022–2023, and from that I was able to write this book. I owe a lot of my success to the decision I made back in December 2019 to just try to create a new private Facebook group for therapists. And I'm excited to share with you everything I know about how to build a thriving group of your own!

When you're building a Facebook group for the purpose of creating a platform for your business, I recommend building a private Facebook group (not a public group). You have way more control over the private group and can approve and decline pending members, you can better protect your group from excessive spam or bot accounts, and you can ask people specific questions upon entry into your group and request their email, thereby building your Facebook group and your email list simultaneously.

Naming Your Private Facebook Group

You'll want to name your group something short, simple, and easy to remember that reflects a hopeful, positive outcome that your clients or customers want to see in themselves or how they envision being. This is why I named my group "Thriving Therapists" and not "Struggling Therapists" or "Surviving Therapists" because who doesn't want to envision themselves as thriving?

Think carefully about who you're trying to attract to your group. What are the qualities, characteristics, pain points, and problem areas of your potential members? What do you want the overall tone of your community to be?

There are lots of Facebook groups out there for therapists, but some have quite a negative tone or are full of therapists' complaints. I wanted a space that was supportive, uplifting, and encouraging. I wanted therapists to come to my group to find inspiration and guidance on how to build and scale their businesses so they can thrive both personally and professionally. This doesn't mean that we don't have posts and comments that at times can share the difficult realities of being a therapist or reveal vulnerable, raw, and honest truths about our industry, but we are generally a very positive place to be and that is by design.

Think about how you would want your group members to feel after learning what you have to share in your community. What do you hope they will experience by being in this Facebook group? How would they describe themselves after being in your group for six months or a year? These questions will help you shape the tone and feeling of your group and help you identify the best name for your group.

If you feel stuck, just select a name and know that you can always change it later. Or select a short name for your group with a longer description or tagline to help explain what your group is all about.

Setting Up Your Facebook Group

Once you name your group, it's time to create the cover photo and set up the rest of the basic structure of your group before inviting people to join it or posting content in it. When you design the cover for your Facebook group, you can include a headshot of yourself, the group name, and the mission or tagline of the community, and add a "click here" image to the cover photo. This will prompt people to click on the cover photo when they join the group, leading them to read the description of your group, which you can edit inside the cover photo.

Under the cover photo description of the group you'll want to keep it short and sweet. Describe who your group is designed for, what the purpose is of the community, and who you are as the admin of the group. Then finally, add a call to action with a link to your website for more information.

You can add the same information to the "about" section of your Facebook group so new members have two places where they can learn more about you and what they can get out of being a member of your community.

Membership Questions to Enter Your Facebook Group

Be sure to create at least three membership questions that prospective members need to answer upon entering your group. Start out the first question by stating "Answers are required for approval," then ask your first question, which should be something that determines whether they meet the criteria for being a new member in your group.

The second question should ask what they need the most help or support with right now. Answers to this question will help you develop content for your group and offers, programs, and services for members.

The third question should be one that invites them to leave their email address to be added to your email list or newsletter. You can let them know that they can unsubscribe at any time, that you'll never spam them, and that you email your list valuable resources, info, and discounts on offers that they might want to be the first to know about. You might even have it set up where as soon as a new member is added to your email list, they receive your lead magnet or opt in automatically or another resource or guide that you've created for them.

The final thing you should do under the membership question section is make new members review and agree to the group rules. Facebook provides you with some standard rules for your group when you build it, but you can edit and add to that list as you see fit. We've adapted and changed our rules over time according to what needs arise in our group. But making new members click that they agree to your community rules is a great way to establish that there are rules for participating and consequences if those rules are broken.

By stating that "Answers are required for approval" at the very top of the list of membership questions, it encourages people to leave you their email address upon entry into your group. But many leave that blank or some write "No thanks" in that space. This doesn't prohibit them from being accepted as a new member in my group, but you can determine whether or not you require their email address to enter.

I'd rather get the right members into my group without obtaining their email address and have them learn about me and my services in my community rather than decline their admission and lose that potential audience member or potential client down the road. If a prospective member meets your criteria for entry and doesn't leave their email address, my recommendation is to allow them to join the group.

Remember, just because someone leaves you their email address doesn't mean (a) they will open your emails, (b) they'll purchase from you, or (c) they'll stay on your list. They can unsubscribe at any time and they do unsubscribe, but that's OK because you don't want to pay for a giant email list that isn't converting for you. You'd rather have higher open rates and fewer people on your list, than a giant list with a lower rate of opening.

You have to work to earn the trust of your audience and earn the right to have authority in your space; it's not guaranteed.

Your Personal Facebook Profile

It's a good idea to add the link to your Facebook group to your personal profile under the info about you so that if people find their way to your profile, they can easily find your Facebook community. You might be wondering how people could find their way to your personal profile. They do that when you comment or post in other Facebook groups. They start by hovering over your name when they're curious to find out more about you, then they go to your profile to discover more information about you. If your profile is public, that makes it even easier for people to find their way to your Facebook group. But if you're not comfortable doing that, you can control the privacy settings on your personal Facebook profile to allow them to see the links you share in your profile or where you work or went to school, for example.

I was very concerned about making my personal profile public, but I ultimately decided to do it for the benefit of growing my Facebook community. I no longer use my personal Facebook profile for private posts.

I typically just post things I wouldn't mind the world seeing anyway. I treat my personal profile more like a business opportunity to allow people to peek into how I live, work, and thrive, which directly supports my brand awareness and traffic to my website or Facebook community.

Everyone has to determine what feels right to them. But the benefits my Facebook community has afforded me vastly outweigh my need for a private Facebook page. If I want to share something private, I use DMs for that now.

Creating Engagement and Content for Your Facebook Group

The keys to attracting new members to your group are consistency and engagement. How do you create engagement? By asking questions that generate longer sharing and longer answers rather than just a simple click of the like symbol or a simple yes or no in the comments under your post. Every post you generate should be an opportunity to get to know your members. Do not simply post something without a question or call to action. If you do, people will read it and keep scrolling and never engage with the post.

You also want to get in the habit of mixing up your posts. Post questions, images, polls, GIFs, and videos, share stories, ask advice, and share your authentic personality in your posts. If you're sharing a website link, remember to share it in the comments below your post. If you share it inside your post, chances are that fewer people will see your post because the Facebook algorithm tends to shy away from sharing website links that might drive traffic away from the Facebook platform. They want to keep users on their platform, which is why when you share an article or resource or link back to your website, you should always write "See link in first comment below" and post the actual website link under the post rather than inside the body of the Facebook post.

Use the topics, questions, and problems that members address in their membership questions as a content generator for you. They will specifically tell you what problems they're having and why they're joining your Facebook group. Use those in your posts. The chances are high that if one member is having this issue, others are too.

Create a content strategy for your posting. Some groups allow sharing on certain days; for example, many groups offer "Marketing Mondays" or "Share Your Social Media Tuesdays." I broadcasted my Facebook Lives once a week consistently for over a year and called it "Thriving Thursdays." My audience started to anticipate that each week I would go live on Thursday afternoons at the same time. This consistency helps your members start to predict when you will be posting certain things, and they begin to anticipate those posts and videos on a regular basis.

Don't be afraid to ask your community what they need the most help with right now. They'll tell you! And you can either provide guidance, resources, and answers, or even programs, services, or offers to solve those problems.

Like email, you want to keep an 80/20 ratio. Share valuable resources and information 80 percent of the time and only sell to your audience 20 percent of the time. If you oversell to your audience before they have the chance to "know, like and trust" you, they might hide your group, snooze it, unfollow it, or leave your group.

When someone comments under your post, you should get in the habit of commenting thoughtfully under their comment, up to the first ten comments in a thread. This will draw traffic back to your page because every time the admin posts or comments on a Facebook group, everyone who's a member is notified, bringing more eyes back to your community.

Shortcuts to Take with Content and Posting

When I was building my Thriving Therapists Facebook group, I would jot down ideas for posts, and at the end of the week, I'd sit down and schedule out one to two posts a day for the whole week at one time so I didn't have to think of individual posts every time I wanted to share something. This helped a lot! You can simply draft the post you're wanting to share, click the calendar icon, and schedule the post right inside your Facebook group, and then it will be scheduled to post at the date and time you select ahead of time. There are also apps and various posting platforms to help you preschedule posts, but some of those tend to get buried in the Facebook algorithm too.

Rachel Miller has a lot of excellent things to share on building Facebook groups. I learned this content calendar trick from her teachings. Fill in this table and you'll have tons of content ideas at the ready. Going down the left-hand side of the chart, make a list of twelve topics you think are relevant to your community, then across the graph list four different examples or ideas you could share about that one topic. When you've completed this chart, you'll have almost a year's worth of weekly themes to focus on for your group with a couple of weeks off for spontaneous ideas you can fill in as you think of them.

Sample Content Calendar Chart

List 12 Topic Areas:	Idea 1	Idea 2	Idea 3	Idea 4
1.				
2.				
3.				
4.				
5.				
6.				
7.				
8.				
9.				
10.				
11.				
12.				

Attracting New Members to Your Facebook Group

At first, your group starts out with no one. How do you get new members to join? You start sharing your new Facebook group everywhere you feel is relevant. You can post it on your personal social media pages and your website. You can invite members to join directly inside the group. You can share it on similar Facebook pages (when and if you're allowed to do so, on Marketing Monday threads, for example).

Then start filling your Facebook group with a few posts and even try out doing a Facebook Live. It's a great idea to practice doing Lives when you only have a few members in your community. That way if you have technical issues or you don't like the way it turned out, you can always delete it without the risk of too many seeing it at first.

Most importantly, join similar Facebook groups and start engaging there in a very valuable way. People who read your posts and comments will find their way to your group by digging into your personal profile and finding the link and description for your Facebook community that you've shared there. Ask questions, create posts, comment, and share in similar Facebook groups. Become the group member you'd love to have in your own group.

You can also ask your new members in your own Facebook group to invite others who might benefit from being part of your community too. Over time, you will find that your group will grow quickly the more you engage with your community, post consistently, and engage on similar Facebook pages.

The most important thing when building and nurturing an audience is to remember that everyone starts at the very beginning. Never underestimate the power of a small engaged audience, and always share and give generously to them.

INTRODUCTION TO SECTION 3

Thriving

The final section of this book is all about how we truly thrive as therapists, blending our personal lives and professional lives to create a work-life balance that feels good. For many years in my career as a psychotherapist, I focused heavily on helping clients become more aware of how implementing really simple self-care and foundational strategies such as gratitude practices, mindfulness, solid communication, and the establishment of healthy boundaries can help us thrive.

I was always amazed at how the most rudimentary concepts around self-care were overlooked and forgotten by most of the people I worked with. Before we ever dove into the reason they reached out for therapy, we would sometimes spend a session or two assessing how they were doing with their sleep, nutrition, hydration, movement, and outlets for stress. Once all of these self-care components were addressed, they typically felt instant relief, and it made it much easier to go deeper into the work they were there to address.

You know how it is when you're sleep-deprived. Everything feels impossible! We cannot think clearly, our processing is skewed, our emotional reactivity is hot, our distress tolerance is low, and decision-making is really hard. Couple poor sleep with high environmental stressors and a genetic predisposition to anxiety or depression and bam, it's like throwing gasoline on a fire! If we can clean up our self-care first and truly tend to our bodies, hearts, and souls, then everything else we're trying to cope with or address doesn't feel as difficult.

How Does Self-Care Relate to Being a Thriving Therapist?

Self-care has everything to do with how we show up for our work, how we feel about ourselves, and our creative potential. It also has everything to do with our capacity for visionary leadership and holding space for big dreams. And it also helps with our ability to stay present and connected and make real change with the people we're serving. Lastly and perhaps most importantly, it helps us feel a much greater sense of joy and happiness and can help increase our quality of life on a daily basis too.

But this section of the book doesn't stop with self-care.

We will also dive into how establishing healthy boundaries helps us excel and achieve our career goals. And we'll also spend some time exploring the topics of creativity, rest, and play and how critical it is that we make space for all three of these in our lives as business owners and entrepreneurs.

Finally, we'll touch on burnout prevention and recovery and end with my final epilogue to you on harnessing your infinite potential and having the courage to do the hard work ahead.

In my experience as a successful business owner, it's critical that we align our business goals with our passions and interests, our gifts and talents, and our truth. I live for retreat work and all things that support transformation and connection. I love building community and helping people realize their highest potential. Being a creative and deeply spiritual person, I love incorporating music, meditation, art making, journaling, shamanic journeying, cooking, dream work, travel, and nature into whatever I offer, whenever I can. Whenever I'm aligned with these passions and interests in my business offerings, they fulfill two purposes for me: they help me feel excited and alive doing the work I love doing, and they easily sell, which also helps me meet my business financial goals too.

If I separated my joy and passion from my work and never included those things in what I do, it would never be as successful. My events, retreats, and summits would likely not even exist.

If you have a personal passion or interest, it's perfectly OK to find a way to creatively blend it into your business offerings. I've worked with thousands of therapists in my coaching over the years, and many of these therapists have a passion for yoga or cooking or wilderness therapy or art making or nutrition, and they've found very interesting ways of folding these passions into their workshops, courses, and retreat offers they're building.

I cringe when I see therapists try to be the gatekeepers of our industry and say we cannot build creative programs or that it's outside of our "code of ethics" to do these things. You can easily pivot to coaching and build wellness models of your company that remove your clinical license from this type of work and free up opportunities to meet the demands of your clients or customers and combine your passion and interest into what you're building too.

Some of the most profound and transformative things I've ever done in my career lived outside the walls of the therapy office.

The most interesting and magnetic programs or offers I've ever seen from other people were also built from a place of deep passion and interest from those leaders. I encourage you to make your business dreams a reality, and I fully support therapists who find a way to thoughtfully weave unique aspects of their being into how they show up in the world to serve their communities.

Now that you've made it through the sections of this book on building and scaling your business, it might feel like you're complete. But do not miss the opportunity to reflect on this final section. In order to truly thrive as a therapist, we need to be sure that the aspects in section 3 are integrated fully into our lives as business owners and entrepreneurs.

I think you'll find this section refreshingly inspirational! Let's dive in . . .

CHAPTER 15

Self-Care

We all know about self-care for caregivers and how critical it is to "first assist yourself and then help your neighbor" when it comes to the airbag analogy on this topic, but in this chapter, I hope to go a little deeper with you and remind you of how critical it is that we establish healthy self-care routines and whenever we fall off, that we find our way back and reset to these core principles again. I believe in this so deeply, I'm willing to say that it's essential to our success as business owners in the helping profession, and too often we don't make these principles a priority.

First of all, you're worthy of nurturing, rest, self-compassion, and deep self-love. Read that again, and even a little louder for the people in the back (of our minds).

You. Are. Worthy.

Once we all agree on this, we can then work to make our self-care practices something we protect fiercely and stay committed to over time. And if we agree that we are worthy of deep nurturing, restoration, and self-love, then when we do fall off, which we will, we can also reset quickly to return to the practices we know help us thrive.

In order to make space for healthy self-care practices, we need to take the time to know ourselves deeply and intimately. We need to know what makes us feel restored and filled up and what types of things deplete us. Are we introverted or extroverted? How do we recharge? Are we highly sensitive, do we thrive on quietude, or do we feel energized when we're engaging with others? Once we know these things about ourselves, we can begin to design a life that feels in support of our optimal functioning. And maybe even more importantly, we can claim what we need in order to thrive and not carry guilt or shame for knowing how to meet our needs.

When we learn to make ourselves a priority, it has a positive impact on everyone around us too. We are then bringing the best of ourselves to every situation, both personally and professionally.

The Big 5

When it comes to maintaining a foundation of healthy self-care practices, I encourage you to review what I call "The Big 5": sleep, nutrition, hydration, movement, and outlets for stress. The first pillar of these being sleep. If sleep is not aligned, it's almost impossible to maintain support for any of the other pillars.

Here's a refresher on best sleep practices:

- Pay attention to what you're doing the hour before you go to bed.
- How you sleep has a lot to do with how you conduct your waking hours. (Are you rushed, anxious, stressed, reactive, or pressured all day long? Then it will be difficult to flip a switch when you go to bed at night.)
- How dark is your room?
- Is the temperature of your room just right for sleeping?
- Where do you keep your phone at night? Hint—it should not be next to your bed.
- Is your phone on silent or turned off at night?
- If you want to get more sleep, go to bed earlier. Don't try to get extra sleep time by sleeping in later.
- Watch your caffeine and alcohol intake.
- If you have trouble falling asleep or falling back asleep, run through a sensory awareness exercise (what do I hear, smell, see, feel, etc.) or try a progressive muscle relaxation or meditation practice.

- Breathwork can help you fall asleep or fall back asleep if you wake up.
- Keep a notepad close to your bed and write things down to empty your mind before you fall asleep.
- Make sure your bed and your bedding are clean and comfortable.
- Invest in the best bed and bedding you can afford! You won't regret it.

After you tweak your sleep practices, take a careful look at your hydration and nutrition. Are you starting your day with a tall glass of water? Or are you starting your day with coffee and tea? It's important to hydrate when we wake up and to make sure we're drinking plenty of water throughout the day.

Nutrition is such a personal experience, and this book is not designed to give health advice on what, when, or how we eat. That said, I think we can all agree that what we eat has an impact on how much energy we have and how our bodies feel. I think one of the most helpful things we can do when it comes to looking at our nutrition is to help bring our awareness back to the present moment.

It's helpful to bring our consciousness to what we're doing when it comes to what, how, and when we're making food choices for ourselves. It's easy when we're overwhelmed and stressed to move into numbing or maladaptive behavior and that can show up in lots of ways. Therapists are humans too! We also find ourselves wanting to escape from time to time.

During COVID-19, I remember aimlessly scrolling through social media unconsciously munching away completely unaware of my body or what my sensations were. I wanted to escape and distract myself from the present moment because my caseload and my life felt so overwhelming to me. I'm sure you can relate. All this to say, if we gently guide ourselves back to consciousness, rather than operating from a place of unconscious numbing, it can help us feel like we're contributing to our self-care bottom line in a positive way.

The next pillar is movement. Again, this is not a book on how exercise will change your life. However, it is important that we find and maintain opportunities to move our bodies in ways that help us feel energized, alive, and vibrant. If for nothing else, movement gets oxygen to the brain and can help us focus on the work ahead. Many times when I am facing brain fatigue or brain fog, I now recognize that this is an indication my body needs to move. I try to pause whatever I'm doing and take a brisk walk outside in the fresh air and sunshine, and every single time I do this, I return feeling mentally sharper and physically energized. I remember on long client load days, finishing with one client, closing the office door, and doing a couple of quick yoga stretches between sessions just to reset my mind, body, and soul.

Whatever you enjoy doing when it comes to movement and stretching, find a way to make this a regular part of your work-life practices. I invested in a standing desk and sometimes take calls on a walk when possible. There are ways to make simple changes and incorporate these into your weekly routine, and the return on investment is very high both personally and professionally.

The final item on our Big 5 self-care list is outlets for stress. What are you doing for fun? What are your hobbies and interests? What do you like to do for recreation, leisure, and play? Most therapists I speak with or clients I've worked with would often laugh at this question. Since we place such a high value in the United States on productivity, it's almost like outlets for stress, rest, and play have negative connotations in our society. Like "Who has time for that?"

When I lived in Europe, I remember noticing a major difference culturally in work-life balance. It has a lot to do with capitalism and our foundational societal differences, of course, but in Germany all of the stores were closed on Sunday, which meant that you were prevented from running a thousand errands all day long and you were somewhat forced to rest or play. Parks were designed not only for children but for adults too. Adults would often be seen hanging out with friends and family at parks on the weekends playing frisbee or soccer, biking, jogging, walking, swimming in lakes, sharing picnics, and eating at beer gardens while their children played with other kids too. Europeans also take a lot more vacation time than Americans do and truly understand what it means to rest and relax.

I remember my European friends sharing really important reflections with me about the American pace and intensity. They noticed that we have a great deal of difficulty just being in the moment. We're always thinking about what's next. We don't know how to unplug and rest or just ease into an unhurried pace, and we don't make a lot of space for play and spontaneous socialization.

When I returned from living abroad, I tried to incorporate some of these concepts into my weekly routines. I tried to protect part of my weekend and not run a thousand errands. I tried to reach out to friends for more spontaneous get-togethers that weren't so hyper-planned out. I took new classes like pottery, art classes, and cooking classes simply for the joy of learning something new and developing a new hobby. I returned to playing my instruments and making art, and what I discovered was a return to joy and freedom like I hadn't felt in a while.

It's not often that highly driven adults who run successful businesses allow themselves to be a beginner at a new skill. But it's such a wonderful experience when we do! It reframes the way we think about facing challenges and solving problems. It helps us feel what it's like to be a beginner again. It opens up new creative pathways of thinking and stimulates a sense of newness that's hard to access without this type of engagement. And it's fun! There are little victories when we learn new skills that feel worthy of loving, childlike celebratory moments of joy.

Permission to Rest

A huge part of caring for ourselves also has to do with giving ourselves permission to rest. This can be really hard to do as an entrepreneur when you find yourself trading hours for dollars and thinking about how you don't get paid time off like other people do. I am guilty of doing this too. For many years, I would work through feeling sick and push myself to show up for my caseload or my work even when I wasn't fully available to. That never worked out well. I would end up leaving with this deep sense of resentment for my work and my clients and that was no one's fault but my own.

Once I started practicing better habits around permission to take time off, permission to rest, and permission to have time to recover from being sick, I learned a really important lesson about how self-love, self-care, and living in our truth give back to us threefold. When we are true to ourselves and admit that we need time off or admit that we need or want permission to rest or heal or not show up to our work for whatever reason that's in front of us at the time, we are actually operating with high integrity to ourselves and our clients. After that period of rest, we find that we're (hopefully) feeling restored and recharged and ready to serve again in our most optimal capacity.

We're also modeling healthy self-care for the clients we serve too. When we share that we are taking vacation time or we need to reschedule sessions from a place of sincerity and truth, and when we acknowledge that we need to put ourselves and our bodies/minds/souls first, we're helping our clients do the same when they're in that same position.

No one benefits when we overextend. Period.

Are there ways that you could help yourself lean into this permission to rest a little deeper? Have you booked your vacation time yet? As an entrepreneur, we need to get into the habit of doing a twelve-month strategic plan every year. The first thing I have people do when we work on this is block out all of their vacation time for the year. That way you can see at a glance where you may need to shift your income streams to accommodate that time off. I used to try to take my vacations when my caseload dipped for the year, which was around the holidays and in August. On the flip side, there are surges in our practice sometimes in January or September when people feel a natural "start" of the new year or a back-to-school feeling of a new beginning.

Aside from scheduled vacation days, you're also allowed to have an unscheduled mental health day every once in a while. And you're certainly allowed to clear your schedule when you need time to recover from illness or injury.

But even on a regular basis, there are opportunities to rest deeper. Not every moment of every day has to be used and packed with productivity. If you want to collapse on your couch and just stare out your window and daydream for a while or flip through a magazine, that's normal and healthy and encouraged. If you want to stay in pajamas on the weekends for hours on end just sipping coffee under your duvet, do it. If you step away from your computer and phone and just close your eyes to give yourself some cognitive rest for a period of time, I celebrate that with you. You get to choose what restoration means for you.

Sometimes giving ourselves downtime or permission to rest brings up feelings of guilt or laziness or like we're slacking off (not being productive). That's OK! Do it anyway. What you're feeling is the pressure from our society and capitalism to only associate worthiness with producing and productivity. Somewhere along the way, we really messed that up! There is enormous value in downtime. Don't ignore the plateaus and valleys. In the spaces between pushing and climbing and achieving, we are investing in resting and rejuvenation. If we don't give ourselves opportunities to rest, we're at risk of experiencing severe burnout, resentment of the work or the people we're serving, or worse, a total loss of our sense of joy, quality of life, and balance.

Listen to the Warning Bells

How do you know your self-care tank is running low or the well is running dry? If you allow yourself to pay careful attention, you'll notice a few warning bells. You might find that your reactivity is shorter or your patience is thin. You might notice irritability, agitation, anxiety, depression, or insomnia creeping in. You might also become aware of your own maladaptive coping tendencies popping up such as numbing, wanting to escape, feeling detached, feeling disconnected, and even noticing apathy or loss of hope. These might sound dramatic, but if they go unaddressed, it's easy to fall down a pretty steep rabbit hole very quickly when we continue to push and push and push without attending to our self-care needs or signs of burnout.

Your Invitation to Self-Care

I invite you to pay careful attention to yourself. Notice your habits. Notice your thoughts and pay close attention to what your body is saying. Where do you feel tension in your body? What is the metaphor for that? For example, do you feel neck and shoulder pain? Are you "carrying the weight of the world on your shoulders"? Are you experiencing headaches or "feeling a sense of the overburdened mind"? Is your stomach off? What are you "not digesting"? Our body can sometimes be calling out to us or screaming for our attention. We've become accustomed to taking a painkiller, ignoring the pain, and forging on rather than listening with compassion, even to ourselves and our bodies or our hearts, souls, and minds.

Bring your awareness back to yourself from time to time and make "noticing" a regular part of your routine so you don't miss these warning signs to rest, reset, or refresh your focus on your precious care of the body, mind, and soul.

Healthy self-care practices go far beyond a bubble bath or pedicure. When done well, they involve a comprehensive review of all things related to optimal functioning. That said, I don't know anyone who maintains impeccable self-care practices all the time without faltering. There are times when we fall off of our best practices and that's perfectly normal and human. The important reminder here is that we don't have to land there; we can hit those bumps and bounce back. If you find yourself slipping away from the practices you know help you feel clear, healthy, and strong, simply guide yourself back with your breath and intentionality.

You are worthy.

I'll say it again . . .

You are worthy.

CHAPTER 16

Creativity & Play

You might be tempted to breeze over this chapter and head to the next one, but I am willing to wager that this might be the most valuable chapter in this entire book, so don't miss it. Tapping into our creativity and play is arguably one of the most important ways we can thrive in our personal and professional lives. Unfortunately, we're programmed to believe that making space for creativity and play is only important up to a certain age in childhood. "Who has the time to play?" is another sentiment we hear often, which only reinforces this idea that making space for play and creativity is a waste of precious time.

What we know to be true is that when we myopically focus only on work, and we don't make space to balance that effort with periods of rest, play, and creative experiences, it quickly leads to burnout. It also makes it incredibly difficult to "think outside the box," generate new, innovative ideas, and dream up new angles and aspects to our existing business products and services.

When we tend to our creativity, it helps us see the world through a new lens. We learn to solve problems differently, we approach things with fresh eyes, we explore the possibility of new, original ideas, and we allow ourselves to consider various options. It helps us move away from feeling stuck or small-minded.

Why Are Creativity and Play So Critical to Our Ability to Thrive as a Therapist?

Creativity and play are critical because therapists are working with complex cognitive constructs on a regular basis. We hold an enormous amount of thoughts, stories, and theoretical knowledge in our minds at all times, while accessing our clients' motivations, insight, body language, affect, their complex history and trauma, the way they process things, and what they're saying, thinking, feeling, and expressing. It's heavy and hard work for our minds.

If we don't feed the other aspects of our whole being, like our need for passion, purpose, artistic joy, music, and sensory pleasure, and we don't feed our heart-centered awareness, and we don't play or move our bodies, run, walk, dance, stretch, expand, explore, or connect, we might find ourselves feeling cut off from living the most optimal versions of our whole selves.

In addition, creativity and play open up channels of energy and key components of integration that are critical to our ability to feed the life and longevity of our career and provide balance between work and rest too.

Seeking Opportunities for Creativity

You do not need to be an artistic person to make space for creativity. Opportunities for creativity exist in our everyday lives, and we can find them in simple everyday tasks. In Julia Cameron's book *The Artist's Way*, she provides a multitude of suggestions on how to discover and recover your creative self. But two of her strategies really resonated for me. One was the concept of morning pages, which is the practice of going directly from waking up in the morning to writing three continuous pages in your journal without stopping. This exercise allows you to essentially download whatever thoughts are flowing through your mind, even the mundane or ordinary annoyances, complaints, or rambling thoughts.

The goal is to get to our innermost hopes, dreams, and wishes, but sometimes first we need to clear out the mental clutter before we discover it. The result of doing this practice on a regular basis is truly profound.

What happens is, when you discharge all of these thoughts from your mind and allow your thoughts to flow, the rest of the day your mind feels open to this unbelievable portal of possibility, and suddenly you have infinite space to think, create, and dream.

Cameron's other suggestion that has always stuck with me was taking myself on art dates for inspiration. This doesn't simply mean going to an art museum, but that can certainly be a great way to fill your cup with creative inspiration. She suggests that the artist who lives within you is like a child who needs to be tended to, taken out, played with, and listened to. She suggests seeking inspiration in nature and the beauty that lives all around us. You could go for a nature walk, visit new and interesting shops, cook new recipes and explore new ingredients, take a drive somewhere you've never been, visit an aquarium or gallery, watch an old movie, or go listen to live music.

Artist dates do not need to be expensive or time-consuming, but when we carve out time on a regular basis to nurture this sense of newness, it moves us from the mundane, monotony of our everyday routines to something more interesting and extraordinary.

Creativity feeds our souls and can move us to feel deep and meaningful connections with ourselves and the universe. Whenever I bring myself to a creative experience, I find that I leave feeling like I can turn everything I know to be true upside down, which helps me believe that anything I want to create as a business owner could also be a real possibility. My neurons feel like they're firing in new ways and that I'm making new mental connections that did not exist before.

Aside from the business benefit, accessing my creative soul helps me feel alive, awake, and uniquely human. I cannot imagine a life without art, beauty, music, great food, time spent in natural spaces, great books, beautiful architecture, and the ability to play. I imagine it would feel very one-dimensional, flat, and lifeless.

Asking "Why Not?"

We live in little boxes. We create these habits and routines that make us feel comfortable, safe, and secure. We tend to buy the same items from the grocery stores, we replace our old jeans with new jeans, and we might even find ourselves vacationing in the same places year after year. And before we know it, we're all boxed in.

Instead of asking why, it might be time to ask why not? Why not buy that colorful planter for your fern? Why not learn to cook something new and different? Why not take a pottery class? Why not get a different pair of pants next time? Why can't you travel to a new destination when you plan your next vacation?

Why not build a retreat for your clients? Why not host a workshop on creativity and play? Why not write a book?

Why not?

I always start to merge back into my own "why not" after I take myself on art dates and explore new, creative ways of approaching things. When I visit modern art museums or local galleries, I get to see creation through the eyes of an artist. I see that anything is possible. That emotion, story, color, line, and texture can be combined in infinite ways to evoke a response in the viewer of that piece of art. I see things I never imagined before. When I do this, I expose myself to original thought and that always helps me break down the mold of believing that there's only one way or a "right" way to do something.

Some of my very best business and personal life decisions were born out of nurturing my creative soul. I hope you'll ask yourself this question too: why not step into a new way of thinking?

Opportunities for Play

Adults need opportunities for play. Incorporating play into our lives gives us a chance to approach problem-solving in a new way. It stimulates our imagination and our ability to think quickly. Play also helps us connect to others and build a sense of teamwork. Play reduces our experience of isolation and can lift our mood. When we play, we tap into a childlike curiosity and wonder that expands our ability to be creative. Play opens up opportunities for risk-taking and strategic thinking in a way that can stimulate new ideas as business owners and entrepreneurs.

But How Do We Do This?

Even if you're not a sporty person, there are a lot of ways to incorporate play-based activities as an adult. I've organized game nights for friends, or supper clubs where everyone cooks together or contributes to a potluck dinner. I've signed up to be part of a women's recreation club in my neighborhood where a couple of times a month, we could gather at our community park to play sand volleyball, bocce ball, horseshoes, badminton, capture the flag, kickball, or other easy sports. I say yes to opportunities to kayak, canoe, hike, or go on bird walks in my community.

Sometimes we need to seek out opportunities for play, and sometimes we need to create them.

I have built creative workshops for women where I organized a different outing each month such as a tai chi night, a yoga night, a pottery class, a cooking class, an art collage evening, a food tour, and a painting class. The purpose was to try new things and give ourselves opportunities for creativity and play.

It might feel silly and unproductive to engage in play-based opportunities, but when we do this, we break down our self-consciousness and open up portals of laughter, joy, and fun without needing to attach to an outcome or result. So much of our lives are focused on being productive and being attached to an outcome. When we play, we're allowing ourselves to live in the moment and we pull away from focusing on the past or the future. You could say that it's an act of mindfulness that enriches our ability to stay in the now.

Think Back to Your Youth

Take a moment and think back to your childhood. What were your favorite ways to play and be creative? What did you like doing when you were young? What kinds of activities absorbed you? Where did you get lost in imagination and your own inner creative world? What kinds of games did you make up with your friends? What was your favorite way to escape? What were the rules of engagement? How did you structure your play? What kinds of play made you feel strong, excited, adventurous, victorious?

How can you tap into these feelings now as an adult? How can you build in opportunities that mimic these childhood experiences? If you did not have these experiences in childhood, how can you tend to those needs now as an adult and safely create opportunities for creativity and play?

If you don't feel like these things come easily, find teachers, classes, organized groups, Facebook groups in your community, recreational sports leagues, music lessons, art lessons, organized camping trips or nature hikes, comedy or improv clubs, karaoke clubs, dance classes, hobby clubs, meetups—anything you can find to give yourself an opportunity to experience the joy of creativity and play.

All play doesn't have to be with others. Some play can be individual play like word games, puzzles, or problem-solving games. There are individual opportunities too like singing or playing a musical instrument, playing handball, swimming, running, walking, hiking, knitting, sewing, journaling, writing, art making, you get the idea!

Bottom line, in order to live a truly balanced life, one that helps us avoid burnout and monotony, we need to build in opportunities that bring us pleasure, joy, laughter, spontaneity, creativity, and enrichment for the soul. When we engage in creativity and play-based activities, we give ourselves permission to imagine other solutions to problems, we stimulate new ways of connecting, and we release steam and intensity from our everyday life. The by-product is that these are all excellent for our personal and professional development too.

CHAPTER 17

Boundaries, Gratitude, Mindfulness

In addition to maintaining healthy self-care practices, there are a few other key practices that help all people thrive, and in this chapter, we will cover three of them: boundary management, gratitude, and mindfulness. When we keep these principles and practices front and center, I strongly believe it reduces suffering, increases our joy, and helps us live our best lives.

Boundary Management

Therapists in general sometimes struggle to set boundaries. We seem to be conditioned to believe that it's our duty and sacrifice to serve our clients at all costs, even at our own expense. That our clients' needs somehow trump our own and that because we have "signed up" to be in service of helping others, that somehow that means we need to always put others' needs first.

This is a recipe for disaster.

If we follow this theory, it will undoubtedly lead to toxic, codependent relationships with our clients where we end up resenting the people we're trying to serve. Let this be a reminder to you that you're allowed to protect your time, energy, resources, output, and investment in your professional life. Know that you are fully allowed to access downtime, vacation time, days off, time off, mental health days, weekends, evenings, personal time, and sick days.

Just because you're eager to build a caseload or eager to scale your business does not mean that you need to sacrifice your life in order to reach your definition of success. The beauty of building your own business is that you can set your own schedule.

When I was just building my practice, a friend of mine said, "I would never want to build a practice because you'll be working all nights and weekends." Honestly, that thought never occurred to me. I always imagined that I would be able to create my own perfect schedule and that building a practice would offer me ultimate freedom and flexibility with my schedule.

It's interesting to note how your vision of how things will unfold has a lot to do with what you create!

Boundary management shows up in lots of ways in our industry, not only in managing our time and schedule. We need to pay careful attention to our boundaries on setting fees for our time particularly with regard to what we charge for cash fee sessions and when we charge clients for no-shows and late cancellations. Many therapists struggle with this, but I encourage you to consider that when you make these policies clear to your clients when they schedule with you, at the start of your first session and in your intake paperwork, it is much easier to uphold your policy and charge appropriately for your time.

At the start of every first session, I always made it clear that "should you happen to forget your session or cancel without twenty-four hours' notice, you will be billed your full session fee." When we uphold these policies and make them clear to our clients up front, we're both protecting the value of our time and schedule and allowing clients the chance to observe how to establish and maintain healthy boundary management without guilt, bargaining, or compromise.

Another more delicate area of boundary management all therapists should be aware of is one that involves our safety as providers. If, for any reason, you feel unsafe working with a client, this should be addressed immediately. If your physical, psychological, or emotional safety is at risk, you have options. Sometimes we experience countertransference with clients and that is worthy of exploring in your own therapy or supervision relationship. But if you ultimately feel that working with a client is no longer safe, your boundaries are being violated by what is being said, how a client presents physically in session, or how a client engages in the therapeutic relationship, it's OK to discuss termination and provide trusted referrals to help transition the client off your caseload or to higher levels of care if required.

Along these lines, it's also OK to determine what you are willing to share or not share with your clients when it comes to personal questions that a client might ask you. Sometimes clients are curious or can express concern if you say you need to reschedule their session. They might ask whether you're having health issues or whether you're going on vacation and where you're going. You can decide what feels appropriate when it comes to sharing these personal things with your clients. This is another way of protecting your boundaries or determining what you want to disclose to clients.

Your role as a therapist might also be challenged in your personal life. Your family and friends may overshare with you at times or recoil and not disclose things with you because they know you're a trained clinician. Sometimes when people ask you what you do at a social event or party, they will have a similar reaction and either try to offload a deeply intimate story in order to get "your take" on it as a therapist, or they may shy away from engaging with you worried that you're "on the clock" interpreting their every word.

It's OK to establish and continue to reestablish your boundaries as a therapist in your personal life. You can keep it light and joke that you're off the clock or you won't bill them for this conversation, or you can be more direct and say that you encourage them to seek the support of their own therapist for these concerns. Either way, you have a right to maintain boundaries both inside and outside the therapy office.

Gratitude Practices

Gratitude can be a powerful practice for reframing our thoughts, feelings, and beliefs about a situation when we're feeling scarcity, anxiety, overwhelm, uncertainty, fear, or doubt, or comparing ourselves to others. Even when we're not experiencing our most hopeful desires (such as a full caseload, a certain income level, a sold-out retreat offer, or any other professional goal we may have), it's helpful to reset by using gratitude practices.

This practice might sound like "Even though my caseload isn't where I want it to be right now, I'm so grateful that my degree is behind me and I'm on my way to building a solid base of referral sources and I'm understanding more each day about what my niche and expertise will be." Or "This retreat offer did not sell out, but I'm grateful I had the courage to step into building this because along the way I have learned so much more about how to refine this offer and make it even better the next time I launch it."

Even at the very start of my career as a therapist, I remember feeling like I didn't have enough clients on my caseload, but when I shifted into feeling deep gratitude for the clients who were sitting before me, the ones I was helping and working with, my entire mindset shifted from scarcity to abundance. In an instant, I felt calmer in my body, I felt less anxiety, less worry and fear, and the gratitude I felt for the client that was in fact on my caseload working with me extended beyond that, and I started to hold gratitude for all of the clients who would find their way to my services and my caseload in the future too.

This practice helped me visualize my full potential.

Through gratitude practices, I could visualize having a thriving private practice, with plenty of clients to serve, with strong trusted referral sources who would continue to refer to me, with plenty of cash fee and insurance clients, and with opportunities to expand and scale beyond that too. Anytime I wavered and felt that fear or doubt creep in, I would center myself, take a deep breath, close my eyes, and extend my gratitude for "what is" rather than focusing on the anxiety of the "what-ifs."

It's easy when we get very busy in our lives and success starts to flow to forget to pause for gratitude. Sometimes we find ourselves so focused on hitting goals and benchmarks in our business that we can't even see the realization that all of our dreams are unfolding right in front of us! I'm guilty of this too.

Sometimes I spend eight to ten months planning large-scale in-person summits, retreats, conferences, and events, and when I arrive at these glorious destinations, I hit the ground running and don't even give myself a minute to look around and absorb the beauty of what I just created.

I've tried to get better about pausing and taking a moment to truly integrate a deep sense of gratitude down to a cellular level when I land in these places. Sometimes I use breath work to bring myself back into my body and help integrate the joy, positivity, and gratitude for the opportunity to show up in the world in this way, to serve my community, and to realize these dreams coming true.

It's well known that gratitude practices lead to joy and joy leads back to gratitude.

What we also know is that happiness cannot be bought and does not live in material things. Many people are chasing happiness in all the wrong directions. When what we know to be true is that joy lives in deep and meaningful connections with others, in our memorable lived experiences, and in our practice of gratitude.

Mindfulness

I discovered mindfulness when it punched me in the gut while I was pulling a load of whites out of the dryer in 2004. Prior to that unforgettable load of laundry, I was knee-deep in a part-time hospital job as a music therapist, I was halfway through my graduate degree at the University of Michigan (UM), and I was raising my two-and-a-half-year-old son. I felt like I was never truly in front of what I was in front of. Anytime I was at school, I was thinking about my son. When I was in front of Elliott, I was thinking about the paper I had to write that evening when he was asleep. When I was at school, I was thinking about work and my patients at the hospital. Consequently, I never felt present or connected. I was highly distracted, anxious, and felt like I was failing in all directions, simply because I was trying to do too many things at once.

At that time, I also applied to present at the European Congress of Music Therapy in Finland and was accepted to speak. What was I thinking?! I was taking an intensive summer course on death and dying at the time, which meant they condensed a longer full-semester course into a short summer session and the workload essentially doubled. In addition, I had to condense that coursework even further to get permission to miss a week of class for the speaking gig in Finland.

I remember preparing for an international trip with my husband and two-and-a-half-year-old child, preparing to present at this large-scale international conference, crushing all of my school deadlines into a tiny time frame, and managing a very intense caseload of patients at the hospital. My head was literally spinning from the moment I woke up until I fell asleep at night.

I left class at UM one afternoon a couple of weeks before our trip, and I remember feeling my legs going numb. I started to lose my peripheral vision. My heart was racing and I started breathing faster. I felt like I was going to get sick. I was sweating and shaking, and I distinctly remember just barely making it to my car in the parking garage where I collapsed in the driver's seat and just started to sob.

It was my first real panic attack and I felt like I was dying.

I called my husband who was so kind to me and offered to drive to UM with Elliott to pick me up and drive me home. But we lived forty-five minutes away from campus, and it felt silly to me to have him do that because then we'd have to go back and get my car the next day. Instead, I decided to try to collect myself and drink some water and I called my therapist. She was between sessions and picked up and walked me through de-escalating to the point where I felt calm enough to drive home.

The next day, I canceled everything and went to see her. I landed on her soft couch where I detailed my overwhelm and she said, "Have you heard of mindfulness?" This was the early 2000s when mindfulness was just hitting mainstream consciousness in the US, and I had heard of it but never really understood the concept fully. She told me that I was feeling super overwhelmed because of what I was trying to accomplish and everything that was on my plate, but she also said it was because I was never in front of what I was in front of.

I was never present or connected.

She invited me to go home that night and truly start to practice bringing my awareness to whatever was directly in front of me and stop thinking about the past or the future and really get into the *now*. I was so used to constantly thinking about what was next that I was missing the deep joy of the moment before me.

She said I truly want you to take a deep breath tonight and whatever you're doing, just bring your awareness to all of your senses and allow yourself to fully be in the moment. Like the good student I am, I went home with my assignment and looked for opportunities to practice this new skill. I hit the door and immediately started making dinner for my family. My thoughts instantly were running ahead to the paper I had to write before going on this trip to Finland. Then my mind was spinning to all of the things I should pack in my carry-on bag to keep Elliott entertained on the long international flight ahead. Then I remembered I had a load of laundry that had to be flipped to the dryer.

I turned the burner down low and ran down to the basement to flip the clothes when all of a sudden it hit me!

I stood in front of the washer and dryer and I could hear my therapist's voice in my head. "Be in front of what you're in front of and bring awareness to all your senses." I opened the door to the dryer and got down low to look inside. I noticed the little glow of the dryer light when you open the door. The way the light hit the piles of white T-shirts and socks. I inhaled the scent of fresh laundry deeply and it smelled so fresh and clean. Then I scooped up the clothes in my arms, still warm from the drying cycle, and I pressed them up against my body to feel the heat on my skin.

How many loads of laundry does a busy working mom do over the course of her lifetime? Millions? And somehow this simple exchange with a load of whites coming out of the dryer is seared in my memory like an unforgettable imprint of presence, connection, and joy.

And why is that?

Because I was practicing mindfulness with such intentionality that in that very moment it felt like the world stopped spinning and all that mattered was the now. Not only did I remember every aspect of this exchange but I also felt a sense of peace, calm, and happiness in this ordinary, mundane task.

From that moment, I was hooked. I knew that mindfulness was a powerful key that unlocked a path to feeling alive, feeling connected, and feeling joy.

Mindfulness is the practice of bringing our awareness to the now, and we can do this with our breath, with our senses, with our intentionality, with our awareness, and with our mind, body, and soul. It's something I've learned to practice on a regular basis, and it has richly increased my quality of life. It helps bring us a sense of perspective that shifts us from a busy mind to a quiet one. It also adds a layer of humility and humbleness, which can help us remember what truly matters when we're feeling pulled in a thousand directions.

We can practice mindfulness anywhere and everywhere.

I often pause and bring my awareness to the moment before a meal, in my morning shower, on little breaks in my workday, out in my garden, while tending to my plants, when I'm in front of my family, at a lovely dinner party, while I'm making homemade soup, while on a hike or a walk around my neighborhood, when I walk to the lake, when I look up and notice the color of the sky. Really anytime I want to reset myself back into the moment of joy that lives right in front of me, I pause to breathe, notice, and experience my sensory awareness, and it always increases my sense of pleasure, positivity, and joy.

How Does Mindfulness Help Us Thrive as Therapists?

Mindfulness helps us thrive as therapists because it's so easy to move quickly from one session or one task to the next and never pause to focus on our momentary awareness. Even in sessions with clients or while hosting retreats, for example, I try to pull my attention away from "what's next" to what is here now. And when I do that, it heightens everything. It intensifies my focus like turning on a bright light or dialing up a microscope. I zoom in on what's happening in real time, and it gives me this simultaneous sensation of both excitement and calm. There's a nirvana quality to the practice of mindfulness that also brings expansion of consciousness and possibility too.

Nirvana suggests that we're in a state of being where neither suffering nor desire exists. Think of that for a moment. To be so consciously aware of your state of being that you want for nothing and feel total bliss, peace, calm, and surrender.

Sign me up!

As an entrepreneur, I'm hardwired to constantly think of what my next move is going to be. It can be difficult for me to relax into the moment. The second my eyes open in the morning, my mind starts running through the list of tasks not only for the day ahead but also the future days, weeks, and months to come. I often return from hosting a retreat or summit and within twenty-four hours I'm off and running to plan the next one! For me, it's exciting to work at a fast pace, but this is why it's even more important to slow myself down and work on living less in the future and more in the present.

I would hate to face the end of my life as a human, a mother, a wife, and a business owner only to recognize that I rushed so hard to get there that I missed the precious beauty of the life that was always right in front of me.

Allow yourself to practice being in front of what you're in front of. Mindfulness matters. And being in the now is where all the rich, juicy beauty and love live. It's also where the very best illumination of creative ideas and innovation is born.

Hit pause and take a breath. Notice what's before you. Even at this very moment. Bring mindfulness to your everyday practices and watch your joy unfold.

CHAPTER 18

I Believe in You!

A couple of years ago, I had a pivotal EMDR therapy session with my therapist. By the end, we had completely rewired the way I thought about one of the most difficult core memories I experienced in childhood. I went from feeling highly anxious and fearful to commanding a new frame—that "I am braver than I know."

It was such a powerful shift in that moment that my therapist told me to write it on a Post-it Note and stick it to my computer so I could see it every single day. Whenever I feel scared and uncertain, I just glance down at my note and remind myself with compassion and courage that I'm braver than I know and that I can face any challenge that comes my way.

I share this with you because I believe in you and I know you can harness the same courage to take tiny steps forward toward any personal or professional goal you have and you're braver than you realize too.

I would like to remind you of a few more things—that the world needs you.

That you entered this profession to make a difference.

That your contributions are so important and valuable.

That if you hold back, it would be such a shame!

So much would be lost.

If you let fear and worry stop you, you'll never know what's possible.

But if you put one foot in front of the other and allow yourself to move closer to your goals, before you know it, you'll be there.

When I got accepted to grad school, I was so excited to embark on my journey to get my MSW degree. I couldn't wait to start! And then, unexpectedly, I discovered I was pregnant. While my husband and I both wanted children, we were surprised by this news and the timeline was not what we envisioned.

My due date was in September, the fall I was supposed to begin my graduate program. I was overwhelmed. How could I possibly start graduate school and raise a baby? With my due date being in September, I knew I couldn't start that fall. The University of Michigan told me that it was not possible to start in the winter semester, which meant I needed to defer my start date by an entire year and begin my degree when my son was one.

I almost gave up!

But I remember my mom saying one of the wisest things she's ever shared with me: "The time is going to go on anyways, so even if it takes you three, four, or five years to finish this degree, you'll either find yourself at that point still thinking about doing it, or you'll be done!" Then she went on to say, "Don't think about the whole degree, just look at the class that is right in front of you."

Much like my wise therapist who invited me to begin practicing being in the moment and incorporating mindfulness into my life, my mom was reminding me to do the same thing. The message was loud and clear. No one eats the entire whale in one sitting. Just put your head down and take a tiny bite of the tail. Don't think about the outcome, just stay present and connected to what's right in front of you and you'll do this.

Opening a Business Is Not Easy!

Especially when we do not have a lot of information in our graduate training on the subject. Scaling that business can feel even harder. But the time is going to go on anyway, so you could either find yourself still thinking about doing these things or you could be doing them if you start now.

I was never ready for any of the large steps I took in my personal or professional life, but somehow I believed deeply that it was worth the risk and that somehow I would be OK even if these things I was trying to achieve fell apart and didn't work.

Again, ask yourself why not?

Why can't you build a practice? Why can't you fill that caseload? Why can't you build an online course, retreat, group program, or group practice? Why can't you write a book or start a podcast? Why not?

I'm willing to wager that the biggest barrier to entry for you might be your own false beliefs. That you're not ready. That it won't work. That it's not perfect yet (PS—it will never be perfect, so please don't wait for that). That you need more training. That no one will come. That it's a silly idea. That you'll feel shame if it isn't a huge success at first.

I've felt all of these things too. And guess what, you're never losing if you start. You're always learning, even when things don't work out.

I opened this book with a difficult memory of visiting my father on an inpatient psychiatric ward. But I want to close with gratitude for that experience. Had I never seen firsthand how deeply mental illness impacts a person's life and their family members, I may never have pursued this career. I'm also grateful that my father has been compliant with mediation and therapy his entire adult life making our healthy and close relationship possible.

I often tell this story when I teach and give talks to therapists. When I was first building my practice, I missed my music therapy world. I had an idea that I should build a music meditation evening for clients and I'd bring my harp and offer this beautiful psychoeducational group on how music can help us learn how to relax. It would be part teaching and part experiential, and I expected standing room only at this event I was creating in my mind's eye.

I had no clue how to build it, so I created a really horrible clipart paper flyer, printed out a ton of copies, and posted them all over town. I hung them up at coffee shops, yoga studios, and the local library. I told all of my clients about this offering and I was sure it would be a huge success. That night my dad invited me to go out for dinner, but I told him I had this amazing group that I was running at the center where I worked. I said,

"Why don't you just come to my program, Dad, sit in the back and when it's done, we'll go out for dinner after." He agreed and met me there.

I loaded up my harp, set up all the chairs in a very large circle, and got the room just right for this amazing night of music meditation.

Then we waited.

My dad and I sat there, looked at our watches and the time went by. I tuned and retuned my harp. Adjusted the seats to give the perfect spacing between each chair. My dad said, "They must be trying to find parking," which we both knew was a compassionate lie and a way of gently saying no one is coming tonight, honey. I walked out to the front of the office to look around to see whether anyone was approaching the building, but sadly no one came. After twenty-five minutes of waiting for no one, I called it.

Time of death: 7:25 p.m.

I was so embarrassed and ashamed and felt like I should just stick to 1:1 work and never try to build anything creative and cool again. That's our natural instinct when we feel shame. We want to recoil and hide. We want to curl up and die with our dreams.

But I didn't stay there long. I realized that my marketing was way off. I expected people to see the flyer out in public without knowing, liking, or trusting me and to just show up on a Friday night for a two-hour workshop that they would pay at the door for. All of it was way off and totally the wrong approach. But if I hadn't tried, I would never have been able to learn these things. I may have stayed small forever.

I might never have gone on to build a thriving career where I get to travel the world hosting transformational and life-changing international retreats. Where I get to coach thousands of therapists on exactly the path to take to build their private practices and then help them build successful offerings outside of their therapy office. And I definitely would have never gone on to form the Thriving Therapists community where I get to lead and inspire others to stretch into their big dreams too.

Can you imagine if I had just stopped there after that first attempt at building a creative offering?

What would have been lost for me and for all those whom I've been able to serve over the past twenty-plus years? What a waste that would have been. I hope this inspires you to dust yourself off and keep building if something similar happens to you.

This book was designed to guide you and provide you with all of the tools and resources you need to build and scale your business, but it was also designed to encourage, support, and inspire you to step into thriving as a therapist.

If you're here with me right now, I want you to know that we are the leaders we've been waiting for. We can't keep waiting for someone else to do these things. Your clients need you and your community needs you too. It's time for you to step forward on your path. It's time to harness your bravery and courage and learn how to sit with your discomfort and uncertainty. It's time to realize that you can't wait until it's perfect. It's time to know that with the right strategic plan in place, your business goals can be realized.

It's also critical that you know you do not have to do this alone!

Unlike when I was just starting out, there are tons of avenues now for support. There are thousands of Thriving Therapists to connect with in our Facebook community. There are coaches like me who can guide you and help you develop a clear path to success. There are resources, online courses, podcasts, and books available to reference when you feel lost and confused about where to go next.

And most importantly, there are colleagues and friends who can be your accountability buddies along the way. I encourage you to find those business besties and share with them often. Share your big, wonderful dreams and ideas. Share your fears and resistance too. Share your blocks and help them reflect back to you how and why you need to move forward. Collaborate and lift each other up. Share with them abundantly and generously and remove competition from these spaces. Celebrate their wins and tend to their wounds when they feel failure. These friendships will uphold you when you feel lost and guide you back to the most positive version of yourself. Invest in these relationships; they're critical to thriving.

Finally, it's time to realize that you are worthy.

You're worthy of freedom, joy, and financial abundance.

You're worthy of peace, prosperity, and security. You're worthy of building a business that supports these goals. You are worthy of self-care and connection. You are worthy of maintaining healthy boundaries in your work and your personal life. You're worthy of play and creativity. You're worthy of pursuing your personal and professional goals. You're worthy and deserve to dream big.

And ultimately, you deserve to THRIVE!

I believe in you and know that you have the capacity to bring forth healing, inspiration, and growth opportunities for all of the clients you impact over the course of your lifetime.

Please don't hold back. What you have to give is too precious and important to keep hidden or undeveloped.

I cannot wait to hear how your next steps on this journey unfold . . .

Keep thriving.

ACKNOWLEDGMENTS

With my deepest gratitude….

To Freeman for believing in all of my wild dreams and forever helping me succeed and soar, your love sustains me.

To Elliott for always casting a bigger vision and for your presence and connection, your grace guides me.

To Hannah for your fearless fortitude, courage and determination, you truly inspire me daily.

To my mom for your positivity, wisdom and love and for always believing that anything is possible.

To Jul who leads by example, never backs down and anchors me in strength and stability.

To my dad for your creativity, your ability to see the good in all people and your love and support.

To Ralph for your continuous care, deep listening and thoughtfulness.

To my aunt Lou for being in my corner, for cheering me on with so much enthusiasm and for always bringing the fun!

To my therapy clients who shaped my understanding of compassion, empathy and resilience.

To the entire team at the Thrive Advantage Group for all the support and good work you do for our clients and their families.

To Meta for selecting me to be one of the Facebook Community Accelerator Award Winners, which afforded me the opportunity to write and publish this book.

To my coaches, Lisa Tener, Brittany Long, Tamara Monosoff, and Becky Barstein. You have lifted me up to a higher level, encouraged me to actualize my biggest dreams and pushed me to flourish as a leader.

To Rachel Miller, without your training on how to build a Facebook group, the Thriving Therapists community would not exist.

To Stu McLaren for your pivotal online course that changed my life and afforded me the time and space to build my own online courses, membership community and write this book.

To Heidi Schindlbeck for your visionary excellence, integrity and joy. I am so fortunate to have you as a trusted and integral part of my team.

To Kym Tolson, my business bestie and soul sister. Thank you for believing in me, cheering me on and helping me thrive as a leader. I cherish our collaboration and kindred friendship!

To Gabi, Andrea and Ashley, your kindness, generosity, love, support and encouragement has carried me through. Thank you for your friendship.

To Jill, Libby, Helen and Elizabeth, for all of the years of hugs, laughter and joyful gatherings—everyone deserves a circle of friends like we have!

To Leslie Duka, my trusted VA who thinks of things I need before I even realize I need them and who makes everything I produce look and feel beautiful, professional, polished and aligned.

To Michael Kent, my photographer and entrepreneurial fire starter. Your images always capture the pure essence of what transpires at my retreats, summits, masterminds and live events. Floor coffee forever.

And finally to you, the Thriving Therapist. Thank you for your trust in me. Your questions and comments in our Thriving Therapists Facebook Community have inspired me, informed me and expanded me in ways I never imagined.

May you forge ahead with courage and passion, lead with limitless potential and thrive in freedom, joy and financial abundance.

BOOK CLUB DISCUSSION QUESTIONS

1. Megan opens the introduction with a personal reflection about her father's mental illness. How has your own family history shaped you as a therapist?

2. When it comes to building your business as a therapist, what part has been the most challenging for you thus far?

3. Which marketing strategy has proven to be the best referral generator for you?

4. Referral network building is critical in keeping your caseload full. Who is your best referral source and how have you nurtured a mutually beneficial relationship with that professional?

5. Do you find it difficult to uphold your practice policies (i.e., late cancel, no show fees, etc).

6. Define your niche and speciality in the language that your ideal client would use to describe their problem or why they're seeking support.

7. Discuss your money mindset. Do you live from abundance or scarcity? Share more about the money stories from your family of origin and how that impacts you today.

8. Have you ever considered building groups to scale your practice? Discuss how you would design these, who are they for, would you have a theme or curriculum, what would your length and price point be? What could attendees hope to get out of this group experience?

9. If you could build a retreat for anyone, anywhere in the world, share what you would build and why.

10. What type of online course does your community need most from you? What do you get asked to teach, share, describe often? How could you monetize this expertise and knowledge as an online course?

11. Do you have a full caseload with a waitlist? Have you considered building a group practice? What stops you from doing this? What fears or resistance do you have?

12. What could you speak about for 30 minutes right now without any preparation? Have you considered seeking opportunities to speak and present on this topic? If not, why not? What stands in your way?

13. What kinds of tasks can you let go of and delegate to a team member? And what types of tasks can only you do yourself as the leader of your business? Do you feel ready to outsource and hire support for your business?

14. Have you considered building a Facebook group or an email list as you scale your business? What type of content do you imagine sharing with your platform? What would the purpose of your Facebook group be?

15. Discuss how you can improve your self-care practices. What areas need the most attention in your life right now? What do you need in order to make this a priority? Time, accountability, energy, financial resources?

16. Megan discusses the importance of creativity and play as an energizing and innovative force in our lives as entrepreneurs. How are you incorporating, or how would you like to incorporate more creativity and play into your life as a business owner?

17. Discuss what you feel grateful for in this moment now. Share and reflect on what is working well for you in your personal and professional life.

18. Megan shared a story about being present with her laundry and how mindfulness practices forever changed the way she lived and worked. Have you had a similar experience? Do you practice mindfulness on a regular basis? How does it impact your life?

19. In the final chapter, Megan shares a story about when no one showed up for her music meditation offering. Discuss a time when you felt like you failed or what you attempted did not work out the way you thought it would. Then share what happened after this. Were you hesitant to try again? Did you harness courage and resilience? How did this experience shape you as a therapist and business owner?

20. Finally, share your biggest dream. What are you hoping to build or create? What is standing in your way? How can you make this dream a reality? What support do you need to make this dream come true?

ABOUT THE AUTHOR

Photo credit: Allen-Kent Photography

Megan Gunnell, LMSW, is the founder of the Thriving Well Institute, a company dedicated to helping therapists learn how to build and scale their practice through coaching, consulting, courses, retreats, and summits. She is the admin of the Thriving Therapists Facebook Community and a recipient of the Meta Community Accelerator Award for 2022-2023. She is also a psychotherapist, group practice owner, international retreat leader, speaker, and author living outside Detroit, Michigan.

Megan is the founder of Elevate, a membership community for psychotherapists, where she teaches therapists how to scale beyond the 1:1 model of care to increase their impact and income. Megan's mission is twofold; to help increase access to outpatient mental health care and help therapists learn how to build thriving businesses without burning out.

She holds a bachelor's degree in Music Therapy from Michigan State University and a Master's in Social Work from the University of Michigan. She has hosted international retreats and summits for over 20 years. She is also the co-founder of Gunnell Innovation where she hosts international food and wine tours with her husband, Freeman Gunnell. She has lived in Munich, Germany and hosted live events across the globe.

When Megan set out to build her practice, there were no coaches, no courses and no guidance on how to get started. She successfully filled her caseload and has worked with thousands of clients. After many years of managing her thriving practice, she found herself at capacity with her caseload and on the brink of burnout. It was this experience that led her to make a significant pivot in her career. She decided to scale her business by building a platform, building online courses, a coaching program and hosting retreats and summits for therapists who wanted to learn how to thrive in their business too.

When she's not busy helping therapists move from surviving to thriving, she enjoys spending time at her vacation home in Northern Michigan, writing, cooking, gardening, and traveling with her husband and two children, Elliott and Hannah.

To connect with Megan, visit www.thrivingwellinstitute.com

Made in the USA
Middletown, DE
01 June 2023